Your Life
IS
Meditation

T0060398

Your Life
IS
Meditation

Mark Van Buren

Wisdom Publications
199 Elm Street
Somerville, MA 02144 USA
wisdomexperience.org

The chapter called "Hope" originally appeared in altered form in *Elephant Journal*.

Library of Congress Cataloging-in-Publication Data
Names: Van Buren, Mark, author.
Title: Your life is meditation / Mark Van Buren.
Description: Somerville, MA, USA: Wisdom Publications, 2020. |
    Includes bibliographical references.
Identifiers: LCCN 2020017805 (print) | LCCN 2020017806 (ebook) |
    ISBN 9781614294498 (paperback) | ISBN 9781614294658 (ebook)
Subjects: LCSH: Meditation—Zen Buddhism. | Awareness—Religious aspects—
    Zen Buddhism.
Classification: LCC BQ9288 .V36 2020 (print) | LCC BQ9288 (ebook) | DDC
    294.3/4435—dc23
LC record available at https://lccn.loc.gov/2020017805
LC ebook record available at https://lccn.loc.gov/2020017806

ISBN 978-1-61429-449-8 ebook ISBN 978-1-61429-465-8

23 22 21 20   5 4 3 2 1

Cover design by Phil Pascuzzo. Interior design by Kristin Goble. Typeset by James Skatges. Set in Tisa OT 10/14.

Printed on acid-free paper that meets the guidelines for permanence and durability of the Production Guidelines for Book Longevity of the Council on Library Resources.

Printed in the United States of America.

This book is dedicated to my children,
Mason Alexander, Madelyn Rose,
and Emmeline Marie.

CONTENTS

Preface xiii

Meditation 101 1

Understanding the Path of Awakening 13

Zen and the Art of Potato Chip Delivery 17

Learning to Open 27

Raking the Leaves of Our Lives 31

Calming Muddy Water 35

How I Ended Up in the Back of a Police Car
on a Silent Retreat 39

Autism and Meditation 45

The Romantic Phase of Meditation 51

The Cleansing Phase of Meditation 55

Positive Affirmations 61

You're Always Free 65

Collecting Mustard Seeds 69

Bowing to Difficulties 73

Every Moment Is a New Moment 77

Post-Retreat Reflection 81

The Present Moment 85

Goals and Meditation 89

Planting a Tree 93

Learning to Be. 97

You're in the Jungle, Baby! 101

Becoming Hopeless 107

When You Wash Dishes, Just Wash Dishes 113

What Leg Pain? 117

The Cracked Buddha Statue 121

A Trip to Nicaragua 125

Breathing: The Anchor for Your Mind 129

Five-Day Western Zen Retreat. 133

Don't Resist the Cold 139

Quieting the Mind 143

Don't Worry, It Cannot Last 147

The Bathroom Door of the Mind. 151

Asking Life What It Cannot Give Us 155

Everything That Arises Passes Away 161

Understanding Buddhist Meditation 165

Why Me? 169

Fertilizer. 173

Motivation from Difficulties 177

The Spider or the Fly 181

Internal Weather 185

Living Beyond Cultural Conditioning 189

Movies with Wisdom. 195

Contradictions in Instruction. 201

The Wisdom of Atlantic City 205

Turning Inward for True Happiness 209

The Wonderful Experience of a Kidney Stone. 213

Health Insurance and Mindfulness 217

Putting Down the Boulder. 221

Meditation and Steadiness 225

The Cave of Demons. 229

The Disappointment of Expectations 233

The Passing Seasons 239

Visiting Lake Pocasset 243

We're Getting Closer to the End 249

Using Mindfulness to Lean into Discomfort. 253

Moving from Subjective to Objective 259

The Viruses of the Mind 263

Beginner's Mind 267

Facing the Walls of Ignorance. 273

Meditation Is NOT Selfish 277

Watch Out for the Tigers! 283

One Body 287

Simplify, Slow Down, and See Clearly 293

Profound Peace at the Grocery Store? 297

The Limitations of Personality 301

The Battle of the Two Wolves. 307

Transforming Aversion 311

Coming Home to Yourself 315

The Broken Jukebox in Your Mind 317

The Pool of Freedom 321

The Waving Crossing Guard 323

If It Arises, It Belongs. 327

A Singer's Last Gig 333

Two Metaphors 337

Birth Contractions 341

Mindfulness and Renunciation 345

Practice Being Kind 349

The Power of Labeling Thoughts 353

Things Are Seldom as They Seem 359

No Self, No Problem 363

The Control Center 369

Practicing with Addictions 373

There Is No Way to Peace 377

In Summary 381

Acknowledgments 389

About the Author 391

PREFACE

FOR ALL OF my adult life (and a little more), I've been practicing meditation, mainly in the form of Zen Buddhism. And like many seekers before me, I began my journey seeking after enlightenment—or at least what I thought enlightenment was. I thirsted for a grand spiritual experience that would free me from my emotional turmoil, from my confusion, from the uncertainty of my life, from all my fears and sadness, and from a monkey mind that just wouldn't quit jumping around to places I didn't want it to go. I was hoping to find something that would essentially save me from my life, from life itself. I felt isolated and alone, and I wanted to experience oneness and a deep, intimate connection with all things.

This way of thinking created a large gap between my spiritual practice and my ordinary life. It seemed as if I couldn't go on enough retreats, read enough books, talk to enough spiritual teachers, or meditate enough times to attain the peak experiences I was hoping for.

A few years ago on a ten-day silent meditation retreat, I realized I didn't need to attain some big experience. And even if there were such an experience to be had, I couldn't force myself to have it—and regardless, it, like everything, wouldn't last. It sure as hell wouldn't save me from being human. As Jack Kornfield says, there is no such thing as spiritual retirement. Eventually you must leave the mountains and come back to the village. And let me tell you, the village is difficult and messy even if you've seen a glimpse of Truth from the mountaintops.

I realized that what I had been searching for all along was an intimate connection to my actual life—and I finally woke up to the fact that I was never separate from it to begin with. How could I be? The oneness I was seeking had been here all along. I was already the mystery of life. I realized I was like a poor man sitting on a bucket of money, or a fish searching for the Great Ocean. The veils were lifted and I saw that the only thing separating me from my actual life was myself, my own mind; what I call small-mindedness. Basically, all the self-cherishing thoughts that filter my life experiences through the narrow hole of *"me, me, me."*

From that moment on, and after many more years of practice, study, and contemplation, I finally understood the direction of a true and mature meditation practice. What I had originally believed to be my ordinary mundane existence was, in fact, my sacred spiritual life. I stopped seeking after some magnificent enlightenment experience, and have instead focused my practice on directly experiencing and working with each moment of my life—as kindly, deeply, and intimately as possible.

Your life *is* meditation—or it can be. I wrote this book to bridge the gap between meditation practice and daily life—but the reality is, there is no gap to bridge. Your practice is always right now, always available. To start to find your way into this, try asking yourself: How am I experiencing this moment? What is this moment asking for? What is my practice right now with these very conditions I'm experiencing? One Zen teacher I practiced with for a while used to say, "How can I meet this moment to bring the least amount of suffering into the world?" Or put another way, "How can I meet this moment to bring the most benefit to all beings?" When understood in this way, every moment is your practice. Every moment is meditation. Practice is precisely daily life, and daily life is precisely practice.

Through the analogies, stories, inspirations, and reflections in this book, I hope you not only deepen your understanding of what meditation practice truly is about, but also find that each moment of your life is in fact a deep expression of it. Although some amount of formal sitting practice is very important and you'd benefit from it every single day, daily life is where your practice is truly and fully embodied.

You may notice the central themes of this book tend to recur frequently throughout—and this is how it has to be. As software engineers would say: It's a feature, not a bug. No matter how long you practice you cannot be reminded enough times to open to the here and now, to be gentle to yourself and those around you, and to practice navigating through emotions and thoughts without getting ensnared by them. I can vouch for this! Even with reminders all around me (some of which are permanently inked into my skin!) I still forget. From time to time I get lost and lose my way. So even though the messages may have similar themes, each chapter will have different yet important subtleties to help you deepen your understanding and commitment to a meditative lifestyle. Plus, certain stories may resonate with you better than others. Maybe a difficult concept doesn't make sense with one story but becomes perfectly clear with another. This is another reason for the various ways of teaching similar concepts.

Don't necessarily try to power through this book. I recommend reading a chapter or two a day—and each day really try putting the teaching into practice. Each day, keep the theme in your mind, and with your whole being, moment by moment, wholeheartedly reflect on and practice what's been taught. Let each chapter's message seep deeply into the marrow of your bones. Become the teachings—no separation.

Truly, you have the power to transform your life—and the contents of this book can help. I have seen what it can do in my own life—and I am no more special than you are. If you practice with wholeheartedness, dedication, and continual effort, you will experience firsthand the liberation this book has to offer. It may not be happiness as you normally understand the word, but more like a subtle and an ever-deepening appreciation and joy for the actual life you are living right now.

I wish you well on your journey.

MEDITATION 101

We don't sit in meditation to become good meditators. We sit in meditation so that we'll be more awake in our lives.
—PEMA CHÖDRÖN

IN ORDER TO understand how your life *is* meditation, I think it would be wise to present the actual meaning of meditation, at least the way I understand it. What is meditation? What are we trying to do when we practice? And why is it important to do it? Is it simply for relaxation and de-stressing? Or is this only the tip of the iceberg? Let's explore some basic concepts.

My standing definition of meditation is practicing being present, or, put another way, making peace with life as it *actually* is. Notice how I didn't say, practicing having no thoughts, or getting rid of things about ourselves we don't like. Nor did I say trying to feel good all the time. If we stick to the definition of meditation as a way to practice being with our lives just the way they are, then there will be no confusion. In my years of sharing this practice, I've seen most people give up on meditating because they "couldn't stop their minds from thinking." Well, here's the good news! You don't need to stop your mind. Your mind is an organ that was made to produce thoughts. This is not a problem—even during meditation. On the contrary, it's quite natural. We don't need to annihilate thoughts; we only need to change our relationship to them. Meditation offers us the chance to *relate to* them rather than *live from* them.

It's also important to understand from the beginning that we are not trying to feel good all the time and we're not trying get rid of the more difficult parts of ourselves. Meditation is never about feeling a certain way, but rather learning to feel and be with whatever arises. I can't tell you how many of my students give up their home practice because they don't feel the way they do when I guide them in one of my classes. Clearly, they are holding on to an idea that a good meditation is one that feels a certain way, and when they sit with themselves at home and

MEDITATION 101 ■ 3

meet an agitated mind, boredom, or any of the other uncomfortable experiences possible while sitting quietly without distraction, they think they've failed, or that they aren't doing it right. It's not that meditation isn't working, or that something is wrong, but rather there are ideas and expectations blocking the practitioner from relaxing into the moment as it truly is.

Many of us also hope that meditation will cure us of our anxiety or depression, or that it will somehow resolve all of life's problems. I fell hard for this one! It's true that meditation has a transformative effect, but it may not be the way we think or hope for. As it is with life, there are no guarantees! Sometimes, after a few months of meditating, people who still struggle with their difficulties feel the practice is not helping. Of course this is not true, but since they have some idea of curing their vulnerable human condition, they suffer when they're staring it straight in the eye. Clearly, any of these ideas associated with these two misconceptions will keep us from relaxing into our lives as they are. We will not always feel good—and that's just the way it is for us humans. We don't need to neurotically try so hard to gain and maintain only happy, pleasant feelings or situations, nor do we need to push the unpleasant away. Is there a different way to experience our lives? Yes! And this is what meditation offers us, and if we understand meditation as practicing being present with our *actual* experience, these misperceptions won't arise.

I'd like to rewind a little bit. Meditation is the practice of being present. But why the present moment? What's the big fuss about our experience right *now*? The truth is, this is it. Our lives are experienced now. There literally is no other time. The past is gone and only exists in the mind as memories. The future is uncertain, always, and no amount of thinking can predict how our lives will unfold, or what tomorrow will bring. Our thoughts about life are never life itself, and this is one of the main reasons we feel so disconnected from it. The storylines we tell ourselves, the memories and anticipations, the judgments and expectations, are all like waking dreams, which pull us away from the immediacy of our experience.

If we understand that this moment is all we have, we can reduce a lot of unnecessary suffering. We don't need to waste time rehashing the past or regretting choices we made. There's nothing we can do about them! What's done is finished! And honestly, there's no use in worrying about what will come, because who knows? It's best to put our effort and energy into just this. Just this is enough for ease. Just this is enough for peace and joy. If you really contemplate this, you'll see that if you're not at ease now, the only place you can be, then when will you ever be at ease? This is it! It's now or never. Please understand this point!

Although many of us may get this conceptually, we need to take it into the realm of experiential understanding. We may understand that this is it, but how often are we actually spending time here? Most of us are so busy thinking about our lives that our actual experience of it passes us by. Last time you walked to your car or the bus or the train, were you present for just walking, or were you lost in your own mind? Did you feel your footsteps? Did you notice the gentle breeze on your face? The blueness of the sky? The warmth of the sun on your skin? Where were you? A moment of your life is gone and you will never get it back. I don't know about you, but knowing that I missed a great portion of my life because I was too busy thinking about it is quite disturbing to me. If we can practice being present, we can gain our lives back, and that is a great gift—and to quote that old meme, maybe that's why they call it "the present!"

As we sit in meditation, practicing being present, what are we actually doing? What is the point of all this anyway? To explain this I break my definition of practicing being present into three aspects: cultivating mindfulness, making friends with what we find, and learning to live beyond small-mindedness.

CULTIVATING MINDFULNESS

Mindfulness is a popular word that's always being thrown around. In fact, I recently saw a cardboard cutout for pistachios with a woman in meditation, hands in prayer over her head, that read "Mindful Nut." With just about everyone using the word, it may be difficult to determine what it actually is.

Mindfulness is typically understood as simply paying attention to the present moment experience, but this is not all there is to it. Ajahn Brahm makes this quite clear with a story from his recent book *Bear Awareness*. He tells of a person who hires a security guard to mindfully watch their house while they go away on vacation. Upon returning the person realizes everything in his house was stolen. He calls the security guard and angrily questions him about his "mindful watching," and about all the items stolen. The security guard replies by telling the homeowner that he did his job. He mindfully watched the house as the robber pulled up. He mindfully observed the robber break into the house and begin gathering all the valuables. Then he mindfully witnessed the robber drive off with all of his nice stuff. Of course mindfulness is intentionally paying attention, but it doesn't end there . . . There must also be skillful action tied to this paying attention while we are in daily life. A hired guard must know who is allowed into the house, and who isn't. So too our mindfulness must help us to observe what's unskillful and unwholesome in our lives and figure out skillful means to not let those parts take over and become harmful words or actions. In formal seated meditation it's quite all right to be like the security guard and simply observe the comings and goings of all experiences, but in daily life, when we are actualizing mindfulness, we must be on guard and only let the wholesome states through!

Besides observing the unfolding of your moment-by-moment experience, mindfulness includes loosening your grip on your judgments, expectations, and labels. Mindfulness invites you to experience life directly, to find out what it's *really* like, and then live fully from there. There's also a sense of warmth that comes with this nonjudgmental observing. We are bathing the moment with loving, spacious awareness. It's as if we are holding ourselves and our lives with the same loving attention we would use as we hold a crying infant. Mindfulness includes curiosity as well. If we think we know how things are, we will never be free. Only by becoming curious will we be willing to go into our difficulties with an open heart and mind. Lastly, mindfulness must be understood as a willingness to be with our lives just as they are. Think about how much of our suffering comes from the thought "life shouldn't be this way?" Perhaps all of our suffering comes down to this resistance. In meditation we take our seat and we sit upright no matter what arises. We choose to be where we are and are willing to be with what presents itself, even if it's difficult or uncomfortable. Being fully where we are is the only way I know to train in making peace with life as it is.

MAKING FRIENDS WITH WHAT WE FIND

Meditation also helps us make friends with what we experience. Normally in our lives when something unpleasant arises, we immediately believe it to be wrong or bad and do whatever we have to in order to get rid of it. Rather than welcoming and befriending the unpleasant experience, we quickly run away. Making friends with the moment teaches us to *stay*. By allowing things to be as they are we are creating a space of unconditional friendliness, which allows us to fully relax into our lives, while also connecting with an inner fearlessness and compassion.

LEARNING TO LIVE BEYOND
SMALL-MINDEDNESS

The last aspect of seated meditation is learning to live beyond small-mindedness. According to the Buddha, our suffering comes from craving, which is rooted in a misperception of reality. This misperception is the belief in a separate, fixed self, which is created by the mind. Essentially, our practice is to learn to see beyond this sense of self and instead live spontaneously and freely. As our mindfulness starts to get stronger, it filters into daily life and we are able to see when we are "self-ing," so to speak. We see when we are closing off, or shrinking our world into the cocoon of "what's in it for me," and we learn to open the hands of thought and let it go. We allow ourselves to soften and respond to life from clarity rather than reacting to it from small-mindedness.

As you go through the rest of this book, and as you continue with your meditation practice, please keep referring back to and reminding yourself of these basic concepts. Your practice is always about being present in this moment, no matter what the content. Throw away your ideas and expectations and simply open up over and over again to what's true—just this! Intentionally pay attention without judgment—and with a sense of warmth, curiosity, and the willingness to be *exactly* where you are. Make friends with whatever you find, and learn to let go of the limiting attachment to self-cherishing thoughts. Eventually, how you approach your meditation practice will slowly become how you approach every moment of your life, and remember, this doesn't mean you don't engage with your life, or choose not to stand up for injustice, but rather you do it from a place of complete presence, clarity, and ease.

If you continue practicing in this way your suffering will slowly melt like snowflakes on warm ground.

UNDERSTANDING THE PATH OF AWAKENING

Whatever precious jewel there is in the heavenly worlds, there is nothing comparable to one who is Awakened.

—BUDDHA

SOMETIMES THE PATH of awakening may seem unclear—and even after years of practice you may find yourself wondering why you're even doing the practice at all. In this chapter, I'm going to offer a metaphor for the essence of the path.

Imagine a stream with no obstructions blocking its flow. The water easily moves downstream, and any extra debris, such as twigs or leaves, is able to freely float on by without getting stuck anywhere. This is the experience of an awakened being. Their life flows, and they flow with it, attaching to nothing that comes through their awareness. Thoughts, emotions, and sensations are experienced, but in a spacious and open way. Nothing is ever held on to. Experience arises and ceases, moment by moment. Right action comes naturally in each unique situation.

Most of our experience, however, is quite different. Instead of an open flow of water, our stream has large boulders in it. The biggest boulder is our belief that our sense of self reflects true reality—this is small-mindedness. We adopt deep-seated beliefs from this sense of an individual, solid, and separate self. Some such beliefs are "I'm not good enough," or "I'm unlovable." These are often our hidden beliefs, which run the show behind the scenes. They're the impulses and drives that run our behaviors, habits, and tendencies. They are created in childhood and are usually formed to avoid some sort of pain we'd rather not experience. These deep-seated beliefs are like more boulders in the stream. On top of these we have the normal thoughts and sensations from daily life—the twigs and leaves. Unlike for the enlightened being, the twigs and leaves don't just float by, but rather get stuck and continue to build up on the boulders until there are piles and piles of leaves and twigs. This ultimately slows down the flow even more until the stream dams up completely. This is the state most of us are in, most of the time.

When we begin meditating, we immediately start noticing the twigs and leaves that have been building up for a lifetime—or longer! Slowly but surely we begin the arduous, repetitive process of freeing up the twigs and leaves and allowing them to float by. Although daily life keeps adding more to our piles, we continue to clean until things become a little clearer. With this clarity we begin revealing the deep seated belief boulders, which are hidden underneath the debris. With time and much patience, we are gradually able to move some of the boulders around. Some we are able to completely remove from the stream, and the water begins flowing better with every boulder we take out. Now, not every twig and leaf gets stuck; some just float on by without leaving a trace.

With many years of continued practice, we keep shifting and removing the boulders, clearing more and more until we finally come to the biggest boulder of all: our own reified sense of separation and isolation—the root of our small-mindedness—the lonely, craving ego. Maybe once or twice in a lifetime we are able to lift this boulder up, allowing the water to flow completely, without obstruction. Although we may never completely remove this boulder, we can push it aside, at least a little, but enough so that most of the stream is clear to flow, and any little buildups can be easily removed.

This is where our practice is leading us.

ZEN AND THE ART OF POTATO CHIP DELIVERY

All I can be is who I am right now; I can experience that and work with it. That's all I can do. The rest is the dream of the ego.

—CHARLOTTE JOKO BECK

RECENTLY, I WAS at the grocery store and saw a cardboard "weekender" display for pistachios. Besides there being images of . . . well . . . nuts (of course), there was a woman wearing all white, hands above her head in prayer. Her eyes were closed and she was sitting peacefully in meditation. I haven't a clue as to what pistachios and meditation have to do with one another, nor how anyone could relax with their arms above their head while meditating, but to each their own.

Meditation has gone mainstream, so mainstream in fact, that companies are now using meditation and mindfulness as marketing tools to sell their products. This is interesting as it shows how we associate meditation with peaceful, healthy, happy, and other "feel-good" types of things. These images and advertisements work subconsciously on the masses, causing them to have many unexamined or half-examined beliefs about the *actual* practice. In fact, my tattoo artist, when hearing about my own intense personal practice, was jokingly disappointed that I didn't float through my house, levitating blissfully from room to room.

As a meditation instructor, I often have to deal with people's preconceived notions and misperceptions, not only about the practice itself, but also with what it means to truly embody it in the messiness of their daily lives. The advertisements and presentations may make it *seem* like another gimmicky, self-help way to permanent bliss, but the reality is much different. Actually, it's not much different from what you're already experiencing every single day . . .

So if embodying meditation is not what the advertisements promote—if it's not serenely sitting on a buckwheat cushion, deep in the mountains of the Himalayas—then what is it? Where does paying the mortgage come in? Traffic jams? Raising children? Working a job you dislike? Continually fixing up a home that keeps falling apart? Standing at the bedside of a family member in hospice? Relationship struggles? And all the rest . . .

Let me share with you what actualizing meditation looks like for me: a husband and father in his early 30s, who works full-time (mostly during ungodly hours) at a job he's not necessarily crazy about, all the while trying to pursue his passion of sharing meditation with the world. Let me invite you for a glimpse into a typical day of my embodied practice. But be warned! It's not going to be what you think!

For starters, my life is not rainbows and unicorns, and I sure as hell don't blissfully float around my house. On the outside, my life may look like the complete opposite of what a meditation instructor *should* be like. But this is my life, and it's the only place I can practice. Where else could I be?

My current full-time job is with a popular chip company. I drive trucks and deliver and pack-out potato chips to food stores. Very Zen! Most days begin for me between 2:30 and 3:30 a.m. Once my alarm goes off, I typically have a moment of angst. It is the middle of the night; most people are sleeping; yet my day is just beginning. I feel the heaviness in my stomach, listen compassionately to it for a breath or two, and remind myself of my practice: *what is this moment asking for*? Usually, the next series of moments go something like this: use the bathroom, get changed, make coffee, and get out the door to drive to the warehouse. I do each one as fully as possible, with as much of myself as I can muster at such an early hour.

During my drive to work I sometimes listen to audiobooks or Dharma talks. Apparently, I'm very contemplative at 3 a.m.! I often find myself deep in "not-knowing" on my short, twenty-minute drive to work. But like all things in life, it doesn't last.

Upon arriving to the warehouse, I smile and greet the few coworkers whose routes have them up as early as me. Most respond, some don't. It's one of the many reminders I get throughout the day that most people don't give a shit about my kindness. My ego cringes every time anyone walks by my "good morning" with stone-cold silence. As much as it pisses me off, and as rude as I feel it is, it shows me with painful clarity the boundaries created when living from small-mindedness. I open my awareness as my insides shut down and allow the triggered discomfort to pass. And it always does.

Once I finally get to a store, I run into the next challenge: the store receivers. They are like the cherubs and flaming sword at the gates of Paradise. Ok, maybe that's a bit of an exaggeration. None of the stores I service are a Paradise, but the receivers are in fact the gatekeepers between you and the store and they have one simple task: check in my product so I can bring it into the store. Rarely is it that easy! Many of the receivers seem to mess with me simply because they can. (After each formal meditation session at home, I chant, *May all beings be free from suffering.* Sometimes with these receivers, I find myself thinking, *How about all beings except this one!*) Sometimes I am able to see through the eyes of Buddha; most times I just get upset. But as often as possible during these frustrating times, I try to return to: *just this.* I touch in directly with the raw energy of my unease, occasionally I'll send out a wish of loving-kindness, and I go on my merry or not-so-merry way.

As the Buddha taught, life inevitably has situations or people we will not want to encounter. This not a problem in itself—if we simply practice *how* we relate to it. The content of life, the *what*, is always what it is at any given moment, just the fact, but it's how we relate to that moment that will either lead us toward or away from more suffering. Easier said than done, of course—but luckily, we have our whole life to practice.

Packing out the chips is a pretty good way to practice Zen, to be honest. Take the bags out of the box and place it on the shelf. Simple enough. For me, packing out is like moving meditation—a way to actualize mindfulness using the contents of my daily life. I don't listen to music or talk to anyone, but instead lose myself in intimacy with the task at hand. If I'm not rushing, thinking of the rude people in the stores, or caught in my head, there is no suffering—just the universe packing itself out! I am where I am, simply doing what I'm doing. Chop wood, carry water, as the saying goes.

Eventually, my workday ends and I drive home to be a husband and father. Usually when I arrive home, my daughter is napping and my son is hanging out with my wife. If this is the case, I eat, shower, and do my formal seated meditation. I find 30 minutes is what works best for me. If my daughter's awake, though, then meditation is on the back burner. No problem—because, after all, my life is meditation!

Although I advocate that people engage in formal practice every day, and I do my best to make it a reality in my own life, sometimes it just doesn't happen. I used to get very angry when I couldn't sit or go on retreat because of life's responsibilities. It seemed as though life would be getting in the way of my practice. I've come to see this is the wrong view. Sometimes you just can't sit. That's fine. Where are you now? Give yourself fully to that. As one of my meditation teachers recently told me, "Your practice now is being a husband and father. Work with that. It's a very difficult practice!" So that's what I'm currently working on!

I wish I could say my day ended there, but typically it does not. I'm home for a few hours before I go back out to work privately with my mindful living training clients, teach yoga or meditation classes, or to run workshops, lectures, retreats, etc. Many people ask me how I do it. How do I go from working at 3 a.m. to all the extra stuff I do? The answer is simple: I do one thing at a time. That's my practice—and it can be your practice as well.

Be where you are. Do what you're doing. If your mind takes you away into a form of suffering or unease, notice that and come back. Practice being present in every moment. Should you sit every day in formal meditation as well? Absolutely—if you can do it . . . even if that means bringing your hand to your heart and taking three breaths right when you wake up. Or you could even try meditating for one minute (about seven to ten breaths) once an hour. If right now your life doesn't allow for either of those, then just practice your actual life. Embody the qualities of meditation every moment: be awake, cultivate mindfulness, let go of thoughts and judgments, make friends with what life presents you, and be willing to be right there with whatever you find. Life will change. So will your states of mind and moods. Don't dwell in any of them.

Ask yourself, how can I meet this moment to be of benefit to all beings? Or put another way: How can I meet this moment to create the least amount of harm? Try your best to live that! Don't worry about getting it right. Don't overthink it. Just do it. Let go into the Eternal Flow, merge with it.

Don't waste this precious life.

LEARNING TO OPEN

Practice does not mean forcing yourself to improve, but trusting your potential to open.

—DAVID RICHO

FINDING PEACE in your life doesn't come about by improving yourself or becoming better, but rather by continuously opening fully to the present moment and working with that. Learning to rest in your ability to be the observer, or as meditation master Ajahn Chah called it, "the one who knows," connects you with a peace beyond good and bad, right and wrong, pleasure and pain, and so forth. As you learn to trust and rest more and more in this spacious awareness, the suffering in your life becomes more workable and less sticky.

So how do you learn to open to your life? Simple! Take a few moments each day to pause and fully experience whatever you are experiencing. Feel body sensations, observe your thoughts and feelings, and notice the sounds around you. Do this without labels or judgments. Try to be with your life just the way it is, rather than losing yourself in beliefs and ideas about how you think it should be.

You can also try to open by fully listening to others. When someone is talking to you, give them your full attention. Don't worry about what you are going to say back, and don't get caught in your ideas about the person. Really listen to what they are saying. Try this with one person today. Watch their facial expressions. Actually *see* them. See what mood they are in, and really try to understand the message they are conveying to you. Not many people know how to truly listen, so you may be surprised what happens when you listen deeply to someone.

Lastly, if you feel ready, you can try to open to a difficult situation in your life, whether it's anxiety, physical pain, a person, etc. Instead of reacting habitually to this difficult thing in your life, give it some space and really observe it, become intimate with it. If it's an emotion or feeling, really explore it on a physical level with your awareness. Instead of trying to get rid of it, connect with the quality of it. See if you can label any thoughts or judgments about it as "thinking," and keep reconnecting with the actual energy, as it's felt in the body. If it gets intense, take your hand to your heart and say, "It's really difficult to experience this suffering. May all people who experience this, including me, be free from it." Most important, with all of these practices, don't have any expectations. Sometimes your bad feelings will vanish instantly, other times they will get more intense or stay the same. Make sure your practice is about opening up to the moment rather than getting rid of anything or trying to get results.

RAKING THE
LEAVES OF
OUR LIVES

*At the moment that I'm raking leaves, at
the moment I'm doing anything, it is my
life, it is all of time, and it is all of me.*
——Karen Maezen Miller

*When you sweep the garden, you are
sweeping your mind.*
——Zen Saying

MANY YEARS AGO, my mother asked me to
help her rake the leaves in my grandparents' yard. I happily agreed and met her there
early in the morning. My grandfather greeted me
when I arrived and gave me a rake to begin clearing the leaf-covered yard. It seemed as though
every time I raked a section clean of leaves, a gust

of wind would blow them right back where they had come from. The whole pile never blew back completely, thankfully, but many leaves would cover over the grass I had just worked so hard to reveal. On top if this, the gusting wind would also put newly fallen leaves in flight, which all seemed to have a direct path toward where I was working.

As frustrating as this may sound, I wasn't upset or angry. I joyfully started raking again and again, and although the lawn never stayed truly leaf-free, it surely wasn't as bad as when we had first started. I knew the whole yard would be covered again the next day, as there were still plenty of leaves in the ash and sycamore trees in the neighbor's yard, yet it didn't matter. I joyfully raked away, momentarily clearing the leaves and placing them in little piles.

At one point an insight struck me like a bolt of lightning, saying this was our job as meditation practitioners—to joyfully rake the leaves of our lives, knowing fully that they will continuously be blown around time and time again. Sure, we may temporarily get a few nice piles, exposing the grass hidden beneath, yet there will always be a few loose leaves blowing around, and at one point the lawn will be covered completely all over again; it may even be as soon as tomorrow, as I'm sure it will be with my grandparents' house.

Rake the leaves of your life with joy, and don't worry if the pile gets blown away or if more leaves come falling down. Just keep raking, joyfully, each and every day.

CALMING
MUDDY
WATER

Muddy water is best cleared by leaving it alone.

—ALAN WATTS

So OFTEN IN our practice we find ourselves trying way too hard.

While we meditate we struggle to bring our mind into the present moment. We hear the instruction "Be here now," but when we try to do it, our minds want nothing to do with it. We dislike this very much. We just simply want to follow the instructions and be good little meditators, yet we keep finding our minds won't listen to our demands. When our minds have no interest in our desire to stay present, we try forcing them to stay, and this, of course, backfires and almost always never works. It's as if we're trying to stop a flowing river. The more you try and dam it up, the more pressure builds, eventually flooding everywhere.

There are two analogies I like to teach when working with people who are trying too hard. One is to imagine our mind as a very wavy pool. Forcing it to be quiet is like taking a huge bat and hitting the water to try to get the waves to stop. Obviously the result is more waves . . .

The other analogy is the muddy water analogy. Imagine a jar filled with water that has mud stuck to the bottom. On a typical day, our mind is the equivalent of this jar being gently shaken nonstop. This makes the water brown and no longer transparent. When we try to force our mind to be quiet, it's as though we are violently shaking the jar, hoping this will make it clear again. No matter how still we get, if we hold the jar it will still be stirring it up to some degree. The only thing we can do to settle the mud is put the jar down and leave it alone for a while. When we do this, all the mud will eventually settle back down, making the water clear once again. It may take some time, but with a little patience our mind will settle if we can just leave it alone for a while.

In fact, we can think of our meditation practice as the art of leaving things alone. Paradoxically, as we stop trying to control and settle our mind, it finally begins to settle down.

Part of the reason we fight our thoughts is because we have a belief that our mind or our meditation practice should be a certain way. Expectations will always block you from settling into the present moment. "In meditation my mind shouldn't be busy." "My mind should be still." "Shouldn't I be feeling calmer by now?" On top of the original few thoughts, which distracted us to begin with, we now begin adding more of them. The frustration builds because it's not going how we think it *should* be, so we try even harder to change the situation, adding even more thoughts. More thinking and more strain equal more waves and more dirty water!

Instead of using this method of force, we can instead try letting our mind be—just leave it alone. Don't react to it or engage with it. Think of the random wandering thoughts like a radio that was accidentally left on, creating a background noise—let's just say for the sake of this analogy that it's a boring, nonsensical talk show. Allow the thoughts to be there. We don't have to try to turn them off, nor do we have to indulge in them; we can rather let it be in the background, allowing each thought to come and go. Eventually the mind will quiet down—or not—in its own time. Remember, the effort isn't in trying to stop the mind, but instead in paying attention in a receptive way to what's actually happening. We aren't trying to get rid of thinking, just learning to relate to it, rather than live from it.

If one thought just will not stop arising, then simply label it. "Having a thought about work tomorrow." "Thinking about the hurtful words my friend said to me the other day." "Obsessing over something I can't change." "Ah yes, my mind is worrying about this." By practicing with our thoughts in this way, our minds will naturally begin to open and slow down, leaving us with a spacious, receptive mind.

The bottom line is that we need to stop needlessly shaking up the jar. Put it down and allow the dirt to settle to the bottom, leaving the water clear and calm, as it once was.

Accept whatever the mind is doing, and let it settle on its own.

HOW I ENDED UP IN THE BACK OF A POLICE CAR ON A SILENT RETREAT

If a tree falls in the forest and it hits a
mime, would he make a noise?

—BRAD WARNER

AS I MENTIONED earlier in this book, for many years of my practice I truly believed if I went on enough silent retreats I'd attain some magical, blissful experience that would save me from all my pain and suffering (and just a quick news flash for you: *no* experience will free you from being a vulnerable and fragile human being). Of course, I eventually realized this was not the case, but nonetheless I still wasted many years trying very hard to attain spiritual highs. During these times of strain and overachieving, though, I found that life would always find a funny way to let me know I needed to lighten up. Here's one example .

At the peak of my crazy search for enlightenment, I decided to run my own personal silent retreat. Since I wasn't yet enlightened, I deduced that my sittings on previous retreats must not have been long enough. I was determined to do my own personal, stricter retreat with multiple, lengthy sittings, without the frustration of a teacher or other fellow retreatants. This seemed like the only logical solution to my "lack-of-enlightenment-experience" predicament.

In preparing for my quest, I sought out many retreat centers in order to find the nicest (and cheapest) center that would allow a broke, eager practitioner like myself a place to stay on personal retreats for varied lengths of time in solitude. After hours of Googling, I finally found the place that best fit what I was looking for, and I locked in five full days and nights (I wanted more but that's all I could afford). The beautiful retreat center was located on an eighty-two-acre chunk of nature in Glen Spey, New York. Upon calling, I explained to the receptionist how I wanted to stay silent on this retreat, and he told me they would make a little sign I could wear around my neck that would let the monks and nuns living there know not to disturb me. I was beyond excited . . .

I showed up bright and early on the first day of my retreat and was eager to unpack and start my intensive sitting. Upon my arrival, a friendly monk gave me a quick tour of the grounds—including a few nature trails—and eventually showed me to my room in a small cabin shared with three Buddhist nuns. I made sure I had the sign around my neck that read, "Silent. Please do not disturb." I then unpacked my stuff and began my self-created retreat. I was on my way to becoming enlightened.

I began my retreat with two forty-five-minute meditation sessions in a row, with only a short break in between to stretch and massage my legs. I then went on to have a vegetarian lunch, which was delicious! I headed back to my room for a short rest to digest, and then proceeded to sit through three more meditation sessions. I did a little reading and went off again for dinner—another tasty meal . . .

After eating, I finally had a little time in my schedule to do some walking meditation and to explore the nature trails shown to me when

I had first arrived. It was around seven at night, and there was still enough light to follow what I thought was the trail, but the dark came quickly and my slow, meditative walk began speeding up. I eventually arrived at two dark houses, which were definitely not part of the trail I had been shown that morning.

I was officially lost.

The light from the meditation center was nowhere in sight, so I had to break my silence and go up to house number one. I rang the bell and waited. A woman hesitantly answered the door to find me, a stranger in all black with a sign on his neck that said, "Silent. Please do not disturb." As I was explaining what had happened, her big scary dog came out of nowhere and began barking at me. He was outside and not on a leash—and I was terrified. But luckily he didn't attack me—the owner called the dog in and it went back inside.

The woman had no clue where the meditation center was and told me to try her neighbor's house. I went to the neighbor's house, and as I got close to the door, I heard yet another growling, barking dog. I guess when you live in the middle of nowhere you need a scary dog to protect you from strange, wandering meditators who are bound to show up at your door. No one was home, which I suppose may have been fortunate—as this dog sounded much bigger, scarier, and hungrier than the last one. I made the short walk back to house number one and rang the bell again. This time the woman's young daughter answered and called for her mom. They wouldn't let me inside (understandably), but the daughter volunteered to search for the number of the center, and I called. Of course the monks and nuns were all in the meditation hall meditating, so no one answered the phone. Just my luck . . .

I was left with no choice. I had to call 911. The emergency call patched me through to the sheriff, who came out with another officer to pick me up. I waited alone outside in the driveway, keeping my eye out for any ravenous dogs.

When the sheriff and his sidekick finally arrived, they looked at me very suspiciously. They asked me who I was, what I was doing, etc. I didn't have ID on me, so I told them I would show them my ID once they brought me back to the retreat center. There I was, alone and cold in the backseat of a police car. At least I wasn't handcuffed!

As they pulled into the retreat center driveway, I could only hope everyone was still silently meditating in the meditation hall. Luckily, I was right. No one saw the police vehicle drop me off. What a relief! I showed the officers my ID and they went on their way. I went back to my room feeling completely pissed off at myself for having broken my vow of silence. How was I going to get enlightened? I had already spoken on day one . . .

Eventually, the only thing I could do was laugh at how ridiculous the whole night had been. Life had once again shown me where I was stuck. After one more day of trying too hard on my personal "intensive" retreat, I decided to go home. Thankfully, they asked me to pay for only two days.

Lesson learned.

AUTISM AND MEDITATION

Obstacles don't block the path. They are the path.

　　　　　　　　　　　　　—Zen Saying

OVER THE PAST four years, I have been working with both children and adults who have autism. I have found this work to mirror the meditative path in many ways. Working with this population is not always easy, and always requires patience, loving-kindness, and compassion. And oftentimes, much like in our meditation practice, the fruits of our efforts are not always easily seen, and the results are so gradual it may seem like nothing is changing. Sometimes, certain things don't change, yet the constant work and effort must go on.

Analyzing and shaping behavior is a large part of working with autistic children and adults. Our goal is to always create functional behavior, while reshaping harmful or aggressive tendencies such as noncompliance, yelling, biting, hitting, and spitting. This goal is very much in line with the Buddha's Right Effort of the Noble Eightfold Path, in which practitioners are to abandon harmful thoughts, words, and actions, and cultivate only that which is useful and in line with wisdom and compassion. It is a slow and difficult process, but in both cases, with the right effort, transformation is possible.

Although there are many methods to shaping behavior, I was taught to use only positive reinforcement, never punishment. For example, during bouts of aggression, I am to protect the student from harm while silently witnessing the behavior. This nonjudgmental *being* with the student does not reinforce the behavior, nor does it give them the negative attention some students crave. In this way, they are not being rewarded nor are they being punished. Instead, it gives them the necessary space to allow this behavior to pass. They soon realize acting out in this way will not get them what they want, and once the storm passes and instructional control is regained, they are rewarded with praise and other rewards, ultimately reinforcing the more adaptive, functional behaviors.

In your practice, you may not necessarily reward yourself for doing the right action, but you definitely can approach your neuroses with a similar, non-punishing attitude. With mindfulness, you observe your thoughts, reactions, emotions, etc., giving them the space to be what they are. When you find yourself in a harmful or destructive state, you learn to sit with it nonjudgmentally, rather than act it out, suppress it, or punish yourself for having experienced it. In this way, you are learning to be with your difficulties without getting lost in them, while simultaneously creating loving-kindness and compassion toward yourself. Once your internal storm passes, or at least eases up, you can regain your own instructional control and act appropriately in that specific situation, thus freeing yourself from your knee-jerk reactions of small-mindedness.

Patience is absolutely necessary when working with autistic children and adults. Shaping behavior is not always easy, nor does it happen overnight. There are many times when I start to notice myself becoming frustrated and have to remind myself to breathe and relax into the process. Sometimes it seems as though the person takes one step forward and two steps back. At times it can be disheartening, yet the teaching must continue.

Similarly, when you begin noticing your own habits, reactions, addictions, and patterns, you may lose patience, quickly dismissing yourself as a hopeless cause. You may find that you, too, take one step forward and two steps backward. This is a natural part of the process. Don't be hostile to yourself for being unable to magically rid yourself of years of conditioning. Instead, take refuge in your awareness—in your ability to know clearly what is happening in your body and mind. Celebrate that you're even clear enough to observe these things happening. I remember many times going to my teacher, explaining how I keep doing the things I don't want to do, and she would respond by saying, "It's great that you're starting to see this." Seeing clearly is the first step to undoing the ancient patterns of our mind, so find ways to cultivate compassion, knowing that all people struggle in this way when they begin working on themselves. Most important, continue practicing, even amid doubts and discouragement. These states of mind and beliefs will pass, as all things do.

Another important part of working with the autistic population is to drop all expectations. Some days I go into a session thinking it's going to be horrible, believing the child will resist me, yet they end up working great for me. Other times, when working with less difficult students who typically never give me problems, they surprise me with all kinds of trouble. It's best to go into each session with a mind empty of expectations. This is very much in line with the practice of meditation.

There is no right way to feel in meditation. It isn't about blissing out or feeling really calm or tranquil. Your meditation practice is only about being with whatever is present. Many people struggle with meditation, saying that it's too hard or that they can't do it. The truth is they have expectations of what it *should* be, but have not yet grasped the concept of relaxing into what *is*.

So whether you're working with autism, living your life, or practicing meditation, remember that it's important for you to practice being open to things as they are. It's equally important to be patient and drop all expectations, because you never know what you're going to get.

Just continue with your practice.

THE ROMANTIC PHASE OF MEDITATION

You can have bliss, but only if you don't chase it.

—Bhante Gunaratana

I REMEMBER QUITE vividly how wonderful I felt after each sitting session when I first began my meditation practice. In fact, the first few times were very exciting. It was as if meditation gave me the ability to see, hear, and feel for the very first time. Colors seemed brighter and more vivid, sounds were clearer, and my body even felt lighter and more relaxed. I generally felt pretty blissed out and was getting more and more attached to these pleasurable experiences.

For anyone who has never practiced meditation before, it can be quite a delightful shock to the body when one begins. Unfortunately, though, meditation will not always make you feel amazing. The difference between meditating and daily life eventually merges, and the original excitement and bliss—if it happened to have shown up at all—will slowly fade away. I call this initial phase of meditation the romantic phase.

It's very similar to a new relationship. You meet somebody new and it's the most exciting thing ever. Both of you are on your best behavior, and you try hard to keep the other person happy. You constantly go out of your way to surprise each other with cute little things, romantic texts, and exhilarating date nights, all the while experiencing warm fuzzy feelings. There is no fighting, and when a conflict does arise, you both adjust yourself, quickly returning to your blissful, happily-ever-after dream world.

Now, for anyone who has been in a relationship for more than a few months, you understand that this phase doesn't last. Eventually, reality sets in, and you both begin to realize the other person isn't as perfect as you once believed. Both of you begin getting more and more comfortable with each other, letting your guard down a bit, and allowing your true self—warts and all—to shine through.

The truth is, after the romantic phase you're both left with the reality, which never meets the fantasies and expectations that were present from the start. The greater the expectations, the more shocking it is when those expectations aren't met. The more the other person is built up to be the ideal significant other, the bigger the disappointment when flaws are noticed.

In the same way, eventually you get beyond the romantic phase in your meditation practice and into what I call the cleansing phase. It's important to understand from the get-go that you will not always feel good when you practice meditation. In fact, you will eventually have to face all of yourself, confronting your limitations and neuroses. Honestly, I believe practice truly begins when you stop feeling good. Of course, that's not to say you still won't feel tranquil and refreshed after meditating, but at times it will be quite boring and not feel good at all. In fact, meditation makes you feel quite ordinary, rather than extraordinary. With this in mind, don't be shocked if after practicing for a while you eventually come face to face with boredom, lone-liness, anger, or anxiety—perhaps often. It's not that you're practicing the wrong way or that you did something bad, but rather that you moved on to a different phase in your practice.

The following chapter explores the next phase.

THE CLEANSING PHASE OF MEDITATION

Meditation is your first habit. Every human should meditate to keep the mind clean. Meditation is nothing but cleansing the mind through a process. You will take a bath so that you may not stink, but if you don't take a bath and you put on cologne, you will stink differently. Meditation is the cleansing of the mind so that mind can tell you who you are.

—YOGI BHAJAN

WHEN YOU BEGIN to practice meditation regularly, it sometimes may feel as though you have opened Pandora's box. All of the unconscious, unfelt emotions and thoughts hiding below the surface may begin to bubble right up. It's almost like opening a soda bottle for the first time; all the little bubbles come rushing to the top. Once you get past the romantic phase and start experiencing discomfort in your practice, you may find yourself doubting meditation in general. You no longer feel the warm, fuzzy, peaceful feelings, but instead begin facing the discomfort and unfinished business of your mind and your emotional world.

This may be a very uncomfortable phase in your meditation practice, but it's important to understand this is only a phase. You can think of this part of your path as the cleansing phase— and you may find such phases occurring in your practice from time to time. Remember, when you start sitting quietly with yourself, you leave your awareness open, allowing your mind to settle away from the normal distractions of daily life. When your mind stills it can finally express those deeper parts of yourself that have been ignored. You may become very angry for days at a time, not really sure why, or you may experience deep, piercing sadness that has no explanation. I know many times I have experienced moments of intense grief, almost as if someone I deeply cared for had passed away, yet there was nothing in my life at that time that would be causing it. Ajahn Chah once said that if you haven't wept deeply many times then you haven't begun to meditate.

The cleansing phase is not only limited to sadness or intense, dark emotions, but may also include fits of laughter, or even peak experiences. When the mind gets quiet, all kinds of strange things can happen. Ajahn Chah spoke of a still forest pool in which he used to bathe. He said that when he sat still in the forest pool long enough, animals would start coming out to drink from it, not even realizing he was there. He also described how, if he stayed still long enough, some of the more rare animals would come out and visit. The animals would stay *only* if he were completely still; otherwise they would get scared and scurry away. He may very well have been talking about his actual bathing experience, but I'm pretty sure he was talking about what happens in meditation as the mind becomes more and more still.

It's important to practice equanimity toward all that arises during this phase, while also training yourself to let go of having to explain everything that happens to you. If you sit in meditation and have an uncontrollable crying fit, there is nothing wrong with you; you don't need to rush to the hospital or check yourself into the loony bin. Instead of believing you are going crazy, realize you are simply waking up. You don't need to explain it, nor do you need to see where it came from. You need only to experience it and let it pass through you like a spring shower.

In this phase, I have found it's best to just experience what needs to be experienced. Give it the space to express itself—and allow it to be there until it decides to go. I've also discovered that once these experiences pass, relief and peace typically take their place—at least for a while.

In the cleansing phase you may also begin noticing your habits, thoughts, and reactions, and it may seem as if your mind is becoming more intense and wilder. The truth is you are finally paying attention to how things really are—how they have always been. The problem isn't the meditation practice; it's that you've never paid enough attention to notice what's actually happening.

Please keep in mind that if you feel as though you're getting crazier, or if you're having strange, emotional experiences like crying or intense frustration, just experience it—let it happen. This is simply the cleansing phase, and once you can let go of some of these deeply held beliefs, emotions, and pains, you'll find that you will feel much lighter. It's almost as if you were carrying around a bag full of rocks and you finally emptied that bag out.

What a relief!

POSITIVE AFFIRMATIONS

I do not believe in any philosophy of positive thinking; nor do I believe in the opposite, in the philosophy of negative thinking—because both are there. The positive and the negative make one whole. My philosophy is holistic—neither positivist, nor negativist, but holistic, realistic. You see the whole in its totality, whatever it is. Good and bad, day and night, life and death, they both are there. My approach is to see exactly what is the case. There is no need to project any philosophy on it.

—Osho

THERE ARE MANY practices that promote positive affirmations. I find them useful and believe they have their place on the spiritual path—but there are many pitfalls when using them.

One trap with positive affirmations is that they can imprison you just as easily as negative thoughts. Using positive affirmations is like repainting the walls of a prison: instead of having dark, dirty walls, you paint rainbows, flowers, and sunshine all over. This may keep you from staying gloomy for a while, but at the end of the day you're still trapped in the prison of your mind—it's just a slightly prettier prison. If you'd like to make your prison pretty, that's fine, but at some point you must walk out of the prison and into freedom.

The good news is you have the key to your cell. In fact, there's no key necessary because the prison doors have never been locked. Try it and see for yourself. Simply experience the present moment from the clarity of open, spacious awareness. Drop the judgments and storylines and experience the freedom of now.

Another trap of positive affirmations is using them to avoid reality. Many people will continue to tell themselves they are happy and at ease, but the truth is they are trying to convince themselves they are not depressed, anxious, sad, etc. In my last book, *A Fool's Guide to Actual Happiness*, I called this "drinking the Kool-Aid." This is where you pretend life is good and that everything is hokey-pokey with rainbows and unicorns. But maybe the hokey-pokey *isn't* what it's all about. Life is certainly not all love all the time. It's not always happy, and it doesn't always feel good, and you know what? That's all included too.

Ultimately, using positive affirmations as a way to take off the painful edge of life is not the way of a true spiritual practitioner. After all, you have everything it takes to face life as it is. You don't need to cover it over with showers of positive thoughts. Now I'm not advocating that you go around being negative and never optimistic. In fact, be "an incurable optimist," by all means, but learn to face your life, as it is at every moment, without the prison walls of your beliefs about it.

YOU'RE
ALWAYS
FREE

When we find freedom, even pain and illness become part of the grace of life, and they are our teachers. Imperfections are part of the display of life. Joy and sorrow, birth and death are the dance of existence throughout which our awakened consciousness can shine.

—JACK KORNFIELD

WITH MEDITATION we realize our own ability to be awake and aware.

When we rest in awareness, we realize that in every moment we have the ability to choose between ignorance and and freedom. No matter how angry we are at someone, if we are aware that anger is present, then we have a choice. Do we pick it up and become the anger—become an angry person—or do we recognize anger for what it is and let it pass through us without acting it out?

This is especially true for anyone with any type of addiction. And remember, an addiction doesn't have to be limited to drugs, food, sex, or alcohol. It could be as simple as habitually reacting a certain way. We could also be addicted to our pain from our past or our worry about the future. Freedom from all of this simply comes from our ability to be aware. It's not something we need to turn on or even think about. We always have the possibility of awareness—but without attending to that possibility, we can end up unconsciously walking through our entire lives. A bad mood pulls to the left, anxiety then pulls to the right, and sadness knocks us down to our knees. For most of us, habitual ways continually run and govern our actions and words.

Yet there is something deeper than this small-mindedness we all cherish so much, and when we rest ever deeper into it, the correct action naturally happens. Of course, we still feel anger and all of these things, but when we rest in awareness, we show up fully to life, seeing the situation clearly, and allowing for the right action for that moment to spontaneously occur. There is a deeper intelligence beyond our desires and aversions—beyond our thinking minds. We only need to let go and trust our deepest wisdom and ourselves.

I know personally that when I'm angry I can oftentimes just let the anger be there, and eventually I know the right thing to do. I usually remove myself from the situation and listen to all the self-justifications and reasons why I'm right. I feel the tightness in my chest and throat, and eventually the fever breaks, so to speak. It's almost like an intense thunderstorm that abruptly ends, letting the sunshine break through. Once it does, that deeper intelligence informs my next move.

Please remember: you're always free. If you ever feel stuck or helpless, just know there is always the freedom to clearly see things as they are, to see everything as the natural, constant flow and change of life. Even if you find yourself in a confusing or difficult situation, the confusion or difficulty will inevitably change. You are never truly stuck, even though it sometimes may feel that way.

Freedom, although simple, is not necessarily as easy as it sounds. You must practice every moment of every day for the rest of your life.

What are you waiting for?

Let go into the deepest part of your being and start practicing freedom right now.

COLLECTING
MUSTARD SEEDS

Don't throw away your suffering. Touch your suffering. Face it directly, and your joy will become deeper.

—Thich Nhat Hanh

There's a Buddhist story of a woman who lost her son and went to the Buddha to see if he could bring her young boy back from the dead. He said he would be happy to help, but first she needed to do something for him: collect a mustard seed from any house in the village that hadn't experienced the suffering of losing someone. Hearing this, the woman went out to the village, exhaustively went from residence to residence—and of course came back empty-handed. It was then that she realized the Buddha's teaching. Everyone experiences loss. Everyone suffers.

In this story, the woman's suffering shifted from "poor me"—this is *my* suffering—to a greater sense of shared suffering. This is something we will all experience at some point. Although the Buddha's wisdom didn't take the pain away, it took away the extra burden of suffering, the isolation, and ultimately the resistance to the fact that her son was gone. This led the woman to open up to her tender heart of compassion, allowing her to understand the suffering of being separated from a loved one, which unfortunately all of us must one day experience.

The wisdom of this story isn't only applicable to the loss of a loved one; it can be applied to any type of suffering. All our suffering is shared suffering. We all have to experience suffering in this life, and the truth is countless others also share some version of whatever problems we think *only we* have. Instead of using our suffering to feel bad and isolate ourselves, we can use it to touch our connection to others and share the yearning to be free. Instead of closing our hearts, we can try to open up, and the more we are able to be open and receptive to our own suffering, the more we can bear witness to the suffering of others, while also helping them to do the same.

So remember, no matter how dark a time you may be going through, there's still an opportunity to practice compassion for all beings experiencing the very same thing. Realize that you will never get mustard seeds from anyone's house, because suffering is the nature of our existence; we all will experience it eventually. Instead of curling up and hiding from this fact, try opening up to it.

Connect with the tenderness of the heart, and be brave enough to hold within it your suffering and ultimately the suffering of everyone. Use this tender heart to spread love, compassion, peace, and joy to all those you encounter throughout the rest of your life.

BOWING TO DIFFICULTIES

To bow to the fact of our life's sorrows and betrayals is to accept them; and from this deep gesture we discover that all life is workable. As we learn to bow, we discover that the heart holds more freedom and compassion than we could imagine.

—JACK KORNFIELD

MANY TIMES THROUGHOUT our lives we come across difficult situations or people. It's easy to mistake these difficulties as blocks to our practice. In fact, every one of these challenges is a pathway to deepen our practice.

It's easy to get caught up in the idea that spiritual practice is only about happiness, love, joy, and compassion. If left unobserved, this idealism can lead meditators into an unrealistic, rainbows-and-unicorns spirituality. It's as if we sweep all the ugly stuff of our lives underneath the rug in order to fit some cultish lovey-dovey concept of what it means to be spiritual. A true meditation practice, though, includes welcoming absolutely *everything*—both the things we like and those that we don't.

The truth is, our brains are wired to completely hate being uncomfortable. We can't stand when someone says something (or when a situation arises) that makes us angry, uneasy, or afraid. We see difficulties such as these as obstacles to our meditation practice, and we try to avoid them at all costs. But it's actually these difficult situations and people in our lives that become our greatest teachers—if we allow them to be, of course. Without a pain-in-the-ass coworker, we would never learn patience. Without the terrible people doing unspeakable things out in the world, we'd never know compassion, tolerance, patience, and forgiveness.

Instead of struggling with or escaping from our difficulties, we can learn to bow to them, as if they were Buddhas in disguise. When life's going well, it's easy to maintain balance, peace, and love. There's no challenge there; it's simple. The real practice begins when things fall apart, or when we get into a really uncomfortable situation we cannot escape from. The world will always be the world, with all of its difficulties and crazy people (including us). Not much will change this fact, but we can absolutely change ourselves and our way of viewing things. By working with the mind that receives life we ultimately transform it. In Buddhism, they say that everyone is the Buddha.

Can we see every person as a perfect manifestation of the universe—a perfect expression of life itself?

We must try our best to remember this, because all the teachings in the world get thrown out the door when things are going wrong. The last thing we want to do is bow to them. But these are the most important times to remember to pay attention.

Try opening up to anything that you believe to be an obstacle in your life, inside or outside, just for today. It can be a disease or illness, a loss, a difficult coworker, or even family problems. The next time you face this difficulty, view it instead

as a great teacher and as an opportunity to practice patience, tolerance, and compassion, and
bow fully toward it with respect and kindness.

EVERY MOMENT IS
A NEW MOMENT

*Every moment is unique, unknown,
completely fresh.*

—PEMA CHÖDRÖN

IN SEATED MEDITATION we continuously try to focus our attention on the movement of the breath. Of course, the endless rush of wandering thoughts produced by the mind breaks this focus quite often. Gently and patiently, we keep letting the thoughts go, returning to the sensations of the breath. If done correctly, we notice a thought has arisen, and we simply refocus our attention back to the breath to start fresh—a new moment to start over.

Unfortunately, many people berate themselves for their inability to keep their mind still, not realizing they can just simply start over.

Actually, we are moving our mind even more the very moment we become upset about it having moved. Our mind is made to think. We will have many thoughts all the time. The point is not to stop the mind, but to learn to notice when it has taken us away from the breath and bring it back over and over again. Every time we come back we have another chance to stay with the breath. At times, the mind may temporarily stop, while other times it may be jumping here and there nonstop. Regardless of what happens, as soon as we notice we've lost the breath, we are able to start over—no big deal.

As we continue with our meditation practice, we will find that every moment is a new moment. This is great news because it means we can always start over. And if every moment is new, this means we ourselves are also new every moment. This can be useful to understand, especially if we have said or done something that has hurt others or ourselves (as we all do sometimes).

Rather than beating ourselves up over something we have done, we can simply acknowledge what we did, and then we can forgive ourselves, and start fresh. We become fully present and commit to trying our best not to repeat the actions or words that brought about the harm in the first place. We are no longer the person who did this harmful thing. Our state of mind is different and we are completely new. Holding on to something we have done prevents us from living in *this* moment, and it also prevents us from acting kindly and compassionately to both others and ourselves right now. This doesn't mean that we ignorantly forget what we've done, or that we don't have to deal with the consequences of our actions or words, but rather that we can practice not getting caught in our emotions and thoughts now, in this moment.

So let's meet the world afresh and start over right now. Whatever we have done is over with, even if it was only five minutes ago. We can commit to trying our best to bring the least amount of harm into the world right now. And if we mess it up?

Good news: we have another chance to try again.

Start over and commit to not making the same mistake.

Remember, every moment is a new moment.

POST-RETREAT REFLECTION

*Don't condemn yourself for being human
and having human flaws.*
— BHANTE GUNARATANA

WHETHER EXPERIENCING body pains, grieving a loss, dealing with past difficulties, or just feeling the suffering of a restless mind and churning emotions, suffering governs our very existence. Sometimes we distract ourselves, thinking that if we stay busy enough, or just get everything in our lives just the way we want it, we may be able to escape this fact of being. Other times we may try to numb out by drinking alcohol, pursuing endless desires, or taking other intoxicants so we don't have to feel the quiver of being. But as we walk ever forward in the path of living our life as meditation, we come to find suffering is just another part of life that doesn't have to be ignored, yet also doesn't need to be feared.

Suffering, like all things, is impermanent; nothing needs to be done to "fix" or remove it. Rather, it naturally passes. The other funny thing about suffering is that most of it is created with our own minds. As Mark Twain once said, "I am a very old man and have suffered a great many misfortunes, most of which never happened." We try so desperately to hold on to pleasurable feelings, thoughts, and experiences, while frantically trying to avoid and escape the uncomfortable ones. We narrow our world by grasping on and limiting ourselves to our beliefs, our hopes and fears, our desires, and so on.

We build our own prison, and the door to that prison is always unlocked. If only we had the courage and fearlessness to step out! Stepping out creates a new kind of suffering, but this suffering leads to freedom, whereas remaining in the same place only leads to more suffering.

I've always understood the idea of compassion—but there's a way this path is revealing that makes it feel like my heart is outside of my body. My heart aches from even the most gentle breeze blowing by. I feel a responsibility to free all beings from suffering by giving them the tools for liberation. Unfortunately, none of us can do the work for any other. We all can do it only for ourselves.

If you connect with these teachings, please listen to that inner calling, don't ignore it any longer, and take your practice all the way to complete freedom of body and mind.

You have this potential within yourself.

Cultivate it.

THE PRESENT MOMENT

Life is available only in the present moment.
—THICH NHAT HANH

THERE'S A STORY about a woman who decided she wanted to become enlightened. She asked all the various spiritual teachers in the area about the best way to do this. They advised her to climb up the highest mountain and go deep into the cave located at its peak. She was told she would find a wise old woman in the cave who could help her

She went on her journey, and after much hardship she finally reached the cave where, sure enough, she found a little old woman sitting in meditation. She bowed to the wise woman and asked for her teachings to attain enlightenment. The old woman smiled and asked the seeker if she was sure that she wanted to attain enlightenment. Of course, she answered yes, whereupon the old woman turned into a demon with a stick and began chasing her, screaming, "*Now, now, now!*" And then, for the rest of her days, the woman could never escape the demon who was always shouting "*Now!*"

This story shows how the key to our enlightenment is found in precise and direct awareness of the present moment. But what is it about *now* that is so liberating? What's the big deal? Why do we need to learn about the now? Why should we practice staying there? What's all this fuss about the present moment, and why is it useful to be fully there?

The truth is, if you actually pay attention to your life, you'll find that it can *only* be lived now, and no matter how hard you try to escape this present moment, it will always be right here waiting for you. The present moment is the only place we can experience and work with our lives. It's where we can speak, where we can act, where we can help others, and where we can choose to not be stuck in thoughts, emotions, or habits. The problem is we have a mind that creates a past, a future, and an endless supply of storylines and judgments—and then takes those things as the truths of who we truly are.

On the most fundamental level, there is simply awareness of the present moment. It's like owning an empty room with no furniture and nothing hanging on the walls, and we come along and fill it up. Now, when we walk in, all we see is the stuff in the room, forgetting all about the empty space that allowed these things to be there in the first place. The idea isn't to re-empty the room, leaving you with nothing again, but instead to appreciate and notice the spaciousness that's been there all along. Everything in the room will come and go, but the space will always be there.

Whether it be getting lost in the past or the future, believing the decorations of our mind—the memories and anticipations—will cause so much unnecessary suffering and will always filter the reality of this moment. Rather than living from the past or worrying about the future, we can instead come into the present moment. This is it. This is the only place we will ever be able to live from. The good news is we only have to deal with one moment at a time. Of course, some of those moments will be highly uncomfortable, but we need only to face one discomfort at a time, one breath at a time.

We come into the now to gain our lives back—to actually experience the immediacy and the rawness of directly touching the present moment. There is something very healing about just simply being open and receptive in the here and now. It is only in *this* moment that we can find out who we truly are and let go of that which we are not.

So we must ask ourselves, do we want to wake up and be free?

Yes?

Okay then: *"NOW, NOW, NOW, NOW, NOW, NOW!!"*

GOALS AND MEDITATION

A good traveler has no fixed plans, and is not intent on arriving.

—Lao Tzu

So often I talk about letting go of the past and future in order to be fully in the present moment, and many times during lectures or workshops I will find there are a few people who misunderstand this teaching and become nervous, confused, or even upset and defensive over this. Typically, the ones most puzzled are the people with strong long-term goals or grand hopes and dreams.

The teaching on being fully present in the moment doesn't mean we can't have goals or strive to get somewhere in our lives—or even in our meditation practice. Ideally we want to be fully in the present moment, because the present moment is the only place that we can actually do anything—the only place where we can live. If we can't find peace in this present moment, then we really can't live anywhere comfortably or peacefully.

We come into the present moment not to get rid of our goals or our strivings but instead to work or act from a place of contentment, accepting that right now *this* is the current situation. If we are fully in the present moment, we can take the necessary actions to get to our goal, rather than getting lost in the hopes and fears about some future time. By being fully present, we can commit ourselves 100 percent to each step in the process of our goals. In fact, we become more efficient because we are fully engaged with where we are.

With that said, it's easy to get stressed and worried when thinking of all the things that may need to be accomplished before reaching our goals. When thinking of every single step all at the same time, things may seem daunting, stressful, overwhelming, and maybe even impossible. Instead of becoming all worked up, try getting all the ideas out on a piece of paper, and from there take it one step at a time, with full dedication to each moment along the way.

Just to be clear: living in the present moment isn't some sort of passive lifestyle where we blindly accept whatever comes our way, without truly engaging with our lives. Remember, we *can* act and work toward our goals, but it's more efficient to come from a mind that's clear and content and dedicate ourselves fully to each step along the way.

This lets us gradually learn to view our goals in a different way. Instead of holding on to the outcome of our efforts so tightly, like "It has to be this way," or "I have to be able to do this," we can shift to, "I am going to give everything I have in this moment, do everything I possibly can to see if I can get to my goal, and if it doesn't work out according to my plan, I will adapt and take a new track." With this approach we give it our all while letting go of the fruits and expectations of our effort.

If we are working toward a certain goal in our lives, this will not conflict with our meditation practice. We should never let the teachings make us feel like we can't have goals or strive to accomplish great things in this lifetime. After all,

I'm writing this book so that I can get these teachings out to as many people as possible. I'm also furthering my training as a yoga and meditation instructor to expand my abilities, making myself better at what I do. I don't just sit at home all day watching sensations and sounds pass through my being. I'm fully engaged with my life, one moment at a time—but without an attachment to a specific outcome.

We must try and do whatever we can right now to accomplish our goals. Remember, if we are always focused on what we want or don't have, or on all the things we haven't accomplished yet, we are never going to have peace and joy in what we do, and we will never complete the things that are going to get us where we want to go as efficiently. As Nick Nolte said, when acting as Socrates in the movie *Peaceful Warrior*, "The journey is what brings us happiness, not the destination."

We can find joy in the journey toward our goals, and we can do it from the acceptance of this moment, wherever we currently are. Whatever situation we find ourselves in, we must work with it.

Don't wait.

Start right now.

After all, there is no other time.

PLANTING A TREE

Act without doing. Work without effort.
                              —*Tao Te Ching*

THE SIMPLE ACT of meditation has the power to transform our lives completely.

It's mysterious how being still for small amounts of time each day can bring about such profound changes—but this is indeed what happens. It's as though the universe itself is working through us, nurturing our body and mind each and every time we sit. Although we may not notice any jaw-dropping instant results, over time we will see how much the practice changes our entire way of being, making us more compassionate, gentle, and wise. It's also important not to get too attached to how quickly results will come in practice. In fact, hoping for experiences or results actually blocks our progress.

Try to think of our practice as planting a tree, starting from a tiny little seed. First we must find a good place to dig. Once the ground is ready and your hole is dug out, we then put the seed in and cover it up. From there the only thing we can really do is water it every day and protect it from animals and too much sunlight. The actual growth of the seed isn't up to us, but instead is up to the universe, the movement of life itself.

Every day we must show up and water the seed, even though for a while it may seem as though nothing is happening. And finally, one day, there it is: a tiny little seedling poking out of the dirt. We now can see all our effort was not in vain, but this small seedling still has a long way to go. It's very vulnerable at this stage of its growth, so we must keep a careful eye on it and continue showing up each day to water it.

As the months go by, slowly it begins getting bigger and bigger. It's hard to notice because we see it every day, but eventually we find that our little seedling has turned into a baby tree. While it's still not as sturdy as a full-grown tree, its roots are firmly in the ground, and it's strong enough to hold its own, so long as no major storms come along. The speed and rate at which it grows is still not up to us. It is mostly out of our control. There's nothing we can do about that except enjoy the mystery of our tree's gradual growth.

As more time passes, it gets even bigger, eventually becoming a pretty solid tree. And with even more time passing, it becomes strong enough to withstand even the whirling winds of hurricanes and other strong storms.

This process is very similar to your meditation practice. We show up day in and day out, sitting quietly with ourselves and our meditation method, and after years and years of practice, we realize it has gradually been transforming our lives all along. We often don't realize it's happened, but it definitely has, and it's still continuing to work its mysterious magic on us.

The most important thing to remember in our practice is to give up all hope for life-changing results. Our job is not to transform ourselves, but rather to water the seed, so to speak, every day. Transforming our lives, becoming more grounded, and having more peace and joy is a process that's not up to us. With time the practice will naturally and gradually bring about these changes, yet all these things are up to the universe. I remember hearing about how, on retreats, Chan Master Sheng-Yen, when talking about enlightenment, would tell his students to "let the universe do it." This is the practice.

As we continue practicing, remember our job is to joyfully show up every day and do the practice. We must unceasingly water the seed of awakening within ourselves. Life will take over and do the rest, but we have to trust it. Before we know it we'll have gone from a seed to an unshakable tree. But don't worry about becoming the unshakable tree; just practice. During meditation, let it all go and be fully present for each breath. Don't be concerned with getting results.

Things will change, but at their own pace.

It's up to the universe, not us.

Relax and enjoy the journey.

LEARNING TO BE

I am a human being, not a human doing.
—Wayne Dyer

MEDITATION PRACTICE is really about learning to be fully living in the present moment. This is it. It's as simple as willing to be here in *this* moment. With a steady daily meditation practice, we show up every day and just sit—not to feel some special way, but instead to learn to be with what is. Some days we're angry, while other days we're happy. Sometimes we're in pain or sick, and other times we're healthy and feeling wonderful. Occasionally our mind is still and quiet, while other times it's an obsessing disaster.

This practice is about showing up, not in order to get better or fix reality, but rather to learn to be with our lives and ourselves with great intimacy, receptivity, and openness. This is the true meaning of practice, and with consistency this openness and relaxed attitude will leak into our daily lives. Eventually we'll realize we have the steadiness and spaciousness that can hold anything that arises, inside and outside, throughout our day. Of course, we'll still have all our neuroses and all the same problems we've had all our lives, but we'll be able to see it more clearly and have a greater ability to just simply be with it and, more important, to respond appropriately to it.

I know it doesn't sound like much but it's true: learning to just be with what is, is very powerful. It really *does* change things, even though it doesn't actually change anything. For me, all my issues are just as they always have been, but with my steady practice I now know how to be with them in an intimate way, allowing them to flow through me. I relate to them, rather than live from them. Of course, I often screw up, but it's natural to not be perfect as we progress on our path. We don't need to give ourselves a hard time about it. We are human and this is just part of the experience.

Thoughts are not the problem, but following, believing, and attaching to them is. One simple technique I once read about in a book by Ajahn

Brahm, which works very well when our mind will not rest in the present moment, is simply telling our mind, *I want to be here.* If our mind goes off into some fantasy or is reenacting some argument, we simply say, *Hey, mind! I want to be here. I want to experience this moment.* It may sound silly, but it is valuable.

As you go through your day today, keep in mind that there's solely this one ever-changing moment. *Now.* This is it. This is your life. More important, realize this is your practice. Whether this particular moment in time is pleasant or not isn't the point. The point is just showing up for it and experiencing it. Let go into *this* moment, and learn to be with it just the way that it is.

With practice you will find you can learn to be open and relaxed, regardless of the circumstances.

You can learn to just simply be.

YOU'RE IN THE JUNGLE, BABY!

The mind can go in a thousand directions, but on this beautiful path, I walk in peace.

—THICH NHAT HANH

IMAGINE BEING taken from our home and dropped off in the middle of the jungle. We weren't given a map or any type of guide to help us survive, and we were left alone with no food or water. For the first couple of weeks, the fear would overwhelm us as we ventured through the unknown depths of the jungle floor. We wouldn't know where to get food or water, nor would we be able to decipher which plants were medicinal and which were poisonous. We most definitely would miss the jungle's subtle signs that would let us know when a storm was coming or when a ferocious, hungry animal was approaching.

As time progressed, though, we would find ourselves slowly becoming more accustomed to our new home. We may not yet know *all* the secrets the jungle holds, but we would at least be able to figure out enough to survive through each day. We'd find ourselves becoming more connected with the jungle as we spent more time alone in it, while also learning many important tools, strategies, and lessons. What once seemed overwhelming and terrifying would simply start becoming part of the daily grind. The more we understood the jungle, the less we'd fear it. The less we feared it, the more at ease we'd become living in it.

With time, we'll learn the laws of the jungle, along with the seasonal changes, animals, and everything else we need to survive. We'll eventually navigate harmoniously and effortlessly through a place that once seemed impossible to survive. Imagine living in this jungle for ten years, twenty years . . . thirty years. How much more in tune would we be with our surroundings? Just think of all the things we would discover and unearth if we spent an entire lifetime there. We would have much jungle wisdom!

Being thrown into an unknown jungle is very similar to the practice of meditation. The jungle in the analogy above is actually our own mind, and the unobserved mind can be a very foreign and scary place. When we first begin meditating and venture inward, we don't know what we're going to find. We have never really questioned our beliefs, reactions, views, or judgments before, so it's quite a shock when we first begin the journey. Many are overwhelmed when they first begin to notice the incessant waterfall of thoughts and hidden, unwanted emotional baggage waiting for them as soon as they sit down. It's quite funny, actually, because when most people think of images of the Buddha or of a person meditating, they picture them looking so calm and relaxed. What is all this un-peaceful nonsense about? It can seem very much like being dropped into the middle of a wild, unknown jungle. But the more we meditate and spend time with ourselves—without distractions—the more at ease we'll become, and the fewer surprises there will be. We'll learn how to deal with aggressive thoughts, cravings, or whatever we might face on a day-to-day basis. Try and imagine one year of observing our mind. Ten years. A lifetime. How much easier will it be to navigate through our lives?

It's important to understand this practice isn't about changing anything. When we get dropped in the jungle, we aren't trying to mow down the trees or kill off all the hungry beasts. Instead, we are learning to adapt to it—to dance with it. In the same way, when it comes to our mind, we don't have to fix it or make it better. Instead, we can learn which thoughts are harmful and do our best to not get caught in them. We will find ways to see greed, hatred, and ignorance within our own mind for what they are, and we will discover skillful means to not become swayed by them.

Similarly, in the jungle analogy we will definitely learn which plants are poisonous. If we see a plant that gives us a horrible rash the last time we touched it, we won't go rubbing ourselves all over it the next time we see it. We'll know better this time! We'll see the danger and learn to walk around it. So it is with anger, aggression, or other difficult emotions and thoughts. We'll know it for what it is, and we'll know what it's trying to get us to do. So rather than suppressing it, or becoming lost in it, we'll just experience it and let it go. But please know there will be plenty of times when we'll just jump right into the poisonous plant, knowing exactly what it is and what the result will be—and that's okay; it's just part of the path. When the rash goes away, we can simply try our best not to do it again.

BECOMING HOPELESS

To say that there is no hope is not at all pessimistic. There can be no hope because there is nothing but this very moment. When we hope, we are anxious because we get lost between where we are and where we hope to be. No hope (nonattachment, the enlightened state) is a life of settledness, of equanimity, of genuine thought and emotion. It is the fruit of true practice, always beneficial to oneself and to others, and worth the endless devotion and practice it entails.

—CHARLOTTE JOKO BECK

WE'VE ALL EXPERIENCED hope, and for many of us, it plays a major role in our lives. For some religious folks, hope may be found in the form of redemption, or a new world order. In the political realm, it may be hoping for a certain president or party to take power, or for major changes to take place in the country. Many times, hope acts as a feeling of security, letting us know things will be getting better.

But there's a subtle aspect of hope that is often overlooked: it is an aversion to or feeling of dissatisfaction with someone or something in this moment, with a desire for that thing to be better, different at some future time.

So, as meditation practitioners, does hope have its place? Is it truly useful? Does it lead to freedom and peace? Or does it rather keep us stuck in the wanting mind? Is the most courageous thing we could do actually be giving up hope? What might it mean to become completely and utterly hopeless, surrendering fully to life as it is in this moment, just as it is. On the other hand, could it be possible to maintain a quality of hope—but with a mind fully at ease with the present situation?

According to the Buddha, the cause of our suffering is *tanha*, typically translated as thirst or craving. This craving could be defined as a movement toward or away from a person, place, or experience. It doesn't include just simply wanting (attachment), but also not wanting (aversion). Whichever it is, both surely seem to be a movement *away* from the direct experience of this moment.

If hope pulls us away from accepting life as it is right now, would it not be considered another self-cherishing thirst? What happens when the future moment one hopes for never arrives? Can we hold on to hope without attaching to an outcome?

Chögyam Trungpa spoke often about hopelessness as a great place to be in our practice. He felt this meant that the egoic mind had given up completely and has finally surrendered to the groundlessness of our situation. Without all the grass-is-greener, fear-based ideas of some other time, some other place, the practitioner can finally focus on what's true—what life is actually presenting them in this moment. Then the question becomes, How do I relate to just this? Or put another way, What is this moment asking of me? Ease and well-being are only possible when we have let go of the hope for something else, and finally settled into the only place we can possibly be—our life in the here and now.

I struggled for a long time with feelings of lack. Much of my life was acting out in ways to cover it over. I tried filling my life with excitement, novelty, and change, trying to maintain a life of thrills. Of course, the thrills would never last and I'd end up exactly where I began. I hoped that therapy, meditation, and spiritual teachers/books would finally help me be rid of this horrid feeling, which seemed to be as ever-present as my shadow on a sunny day. I wasted many years hoping not to feel the way I was in fact feeling. There was never any peace.

At some point, it clicked. What I was feeling was clearly not going anywhere, and all attempts to cover it up or remove it were futile (and actually seemed to make it worse). Finally, I came to a moment of hopelessness. Maybe this is a part of me I will have to experience the rest of my life, I thought. Maybe this won't go away. And then, at that moment, peace became a possibility. I was no longer warring with this painful aspect of myself, but rather was trying to understand how to make friends with it.

I decided to begin practicing a path of "how to *relate to* this" rather than one of "how can I *get rid of* this"—and in giving up the hope that my suffering will go away, I was able to turn toward it, make friends with it, and ultimately find peace within it. I was no longer living life from my sense of lack, but instead relating to it with warm, compassionate attention. Paradoxically, when I stopped trying to get rid of it, it slowly began to go away. This is often the way it goes—but there's no way to circumvent that first step of true hopelessness and surrender.

In my situation hope had actually blocked me from transforming my suffering—but does this mean we have to abandon hope all together? According to Norman Fischer, perhaps not. In his book *Solid Ground: Buddhist Wisdom for Difficult Times*, he writes: "Accepting suffering as part of our lives doesn't mean we give up hope or stop wanting some things to be different. For example, if someone we love is diagnosed with cancer, of course we will hope and search for a cure. We can accept the fact of the diagnosis at the same time that we do everything possible to ameliorate it. Acceptance is not resignation. Acceptance is a lively engagement with conditions as they are."

Perhaps then hope *is* possible, as long as it is a "lively engagement" from a place of acceptance, rather than a desperate attachment to an outcome.

Whether we hope or not, one thing is certain . . . whatever life is presenting us is the reality of the moment, and our hopes for life to be other than what it is has the potential to pull us away from that. We may be able to hold on to hope while fully accepting the present experience, but I ask you to consider, even for only one breath, becoming completely hopeless—and letting go fully into your life just the way it is right now.

WHEN YOU WASH DISHES, JUST WASH DISHES

To my mind, the idea that doing dishes is unpleasant can occur only when you aren't doing them . . . The dishes themselves and that fact that I am here washing them are miracles!

—THICH NHAT HANH

FOR MOST OF MY LIFE, I couldn't stand washing the dishes.

I had been spoiled with a dishwasher—and also with a mother who would clean up after me. No matter how motivated I thought I was to help out, I just couldn't get myself to do it. I didn't like getting wet and soapy, and I had even more trouble touching other people's used utensils and plates. The worst part was cleaning the sink of all the leftover food bits after the dishes were done. Yuck. The last thing I would ever be caught dead doing was washing the dishes.

I saw my aversion to washing dishes clearly when I moved into an apartment with a close friend. Neither my roommate nor I ever wanted to do the dishes. At times, piles and piles of dishes would build up, creating an ever-worsening avoidance of the sink. We cleaned them only when the smell got so bad that we couldn't take it anymore. We disliked washing our dishes so much that we eventually learned to use one dish and leave it in the sink until we wanted to eat again. When it was time for our next meal, we would quickly do a half-assed cleaning job on that dish and use it again. Most of the time we just rinsed it with hot water instead of using soap. Hot water kills germs just like soap, right?

The second place where I really dove headfirst into this aversion was at Dharma Drum Retreat Center on my long, intensive retreats. On retreats, every participant is assigned a work-practice job, where the practice of meditation is applied to an everyday job. Every time I went there, though, I always seemed to end up being the damn dishwasher (that or the toilet cleaner . . . but that's another story for another time). I spent many cleaning sessions grumpily scrubbing away at the dirty dishes. Luckily, at the retreat center, everyone is told to clean their plate with hot water and drink the leftovers, so *most* of the plates were clean—at least the plates of the practitioners who followed the rules.

It wasn't until I realized that every single part of life is practice that I could finally appreciate and look forward to washing the dishes. As far as the dishes were concerned, the practice was simple: *Be where you are. Fully be there.* I tried this out. I rolled up my sleeves, turned on the water, and experienced fully, without judgment, the act of cleaning the dishes. I felt the sensations of the plate in one hand, and the sponge in the other. I listened intently to the sounds of the water pouring into the sink. I sensed each muscle that helped me with the cleaning motion expanding and contracting. I felt each swipe of the sponge on every dish. It was actually quite relaxing. In fact, since that time I have had no problem cleaning the dishes. I actually enjoy it when I get stuck cleaning up after meals.

The next time the dishes are dirty, try volunteering to wash them, especially if there's an aversion to doing so. Think of other activities or situations that may be seemingly unpleasant as well, and apply the same teaching to them.

Be fully present and see if the chore can be transformed by letting go of judgments and fully experiencing the task at hand.

Good luck—and happy cleaning.

WHAT LEG PAIN?

Pain is inevitable; suffering is optional.
                    —BUDDHIST PROVERB

ALLOWING THINGS TO be as they are can be a very profound and powerful practice.

One example of this is from my own experience on long meditation retreats. On these retreats much time can be spent meditating. On average, retreatants end up sitting cross-legged somewhere between six to eight hours a day, and I'll tell you this, there are no magical, special cushions or anything else to make it more comfortable. Try sitting in meditation for five minutes on a cushion on the floor, and can see how uncomfortable it can get.

On these retreats, there is potential for immense suffering, yet there is a difference between pain and suffering. Pain is inevitable.

We have a body that has a nervous system, so sometimes things are going to hurt. The suffering is all the extra mental anguish we throw on top. "Life shouldn't be this way." "Life should be some other way." "I shouldn't feel this." "This shouldn't have happened." As scary and as painful as it is to sometimes face reality, we always have the ability to allow *what is* to be there, connecting us with an inherent spaciousness. Right there, smack in the middle of the pain, we can find peace. Or rather, we can *be* peace.

When I'm sitting there in meditation on retreat in excruciating pain, I really have two options: sit there and let it hurt and relax as best as I can, or try to move my leg a little and shift around, doing anything in my power to escape the discomfort. I have found that as soon as I shift my body to get more comfortable, I have already identified with the pain and the aversion to that pain. I believe that this is *my* leg and *my* pain. Only then does it become a problem. As soon as I move an inch to be free from the pain, it sets me up for a torturous meditation period. When I become the leg pain, it seems as though the bell to end the session never comes—which then makes me mad. Then this anger colors my reality, and I get pissed at the guy next to me for breathing too loudly. All of a sudden I'm pissed off at the world, and it seems like I've been sitting there for three hours. All of this because I decided to move that one little inch to get myself to be a little more comfortable.

But when I just sit with it, yes, it's still going to be very uncomfortable, but that's it. That's all it can do—be uncomfortable. And if I have a nice wide-open awareness, it's just one thing among the many things happening in that moment. I don't have to let my mind dwell only on the painful parts. When I allow the leg pain to be there, the meditation period is fine. The bell rings and I am able to stretch my leg out, relieving the initial pain. Just like that, the unbearable pain is gone.

Having this knowledge of how to deal with pain, we can try bringing this into our lives.

If there is any physical pain experienced today, just try to let it to be there.

Don't make a big deal out of it; just let it be, and see what happens.

THE CRACKED
BUDDHA STATUE

Nothing we see or hear is perfect. But right there in the imperfection is perfect reality.

—SHUNRYU SUZUKI

I HAVE A small obsession with collecting Buddha statues.

I currently have well over a dozen Buddhas, some plastic, some wood, all varying in size, color, and style. I tend to blame the statues for my purchases, as I've always felt they actually pick me. Once one of those little Buddhas captures my eye, I can't seem to say no to taking it home. So much for letting go of desires . . .

I recently visited my cousin and his wife, who live out in Hunterdon County, New Jersey. Of course, being the sucker that I am for Buddha statues, I couldn't help but visit my favorite statue supply store, Two Buttons. Two Buttons is owned by Elizabeth Gilbert, the author of *Eat, Pray, Love*, and is a store filled with tons and tons of statues, clothing, art, and jewelry from her travels around the world. It is an Eastern culture goldmine for collectors like me.

I walked through the store for a good thirty minutes, trying to find the newest piece for my collection. Out of the hundreds of statues, only two or three were reaching out to me. My wife, who already thinks I have enough statues, told me I could get only one. In the interest of marital harmony, I accepted this. The good news was that I had a hundred-dollar gift card from Christmas and found out everything in the store was 50 percent off for a very limited time. With that knowledge, I was on a mission to buy a nice expensive piece.

One particular Buddha was made of a nice heavy wood and had a beautifully carved face and body. It was stained, with a nice dark-colored finish to top it off. But there were two cracks in the leg, which made me hesitant to buy it. I walked back and forth between the three statues, staring intently at each one. The two other crack-free Buddhas were nice, but the face of the cracked one really took hold of me. I mustered up the courage to temporarily let go of this flaw, and I brought this Buddha home with me.

Although I loved the statue very much, from the time I purchased it until weeks after, my mind kept obsessing over the two cracks. I kept debating whether or not I should fix it or try to glue it to prevent further cracking. An endless flow of thoughts rushed through my head every time I saw or thought about the statue. I was getting more and more anxious about my little cracked wooden Buddha. I even found myself telling people about the crack. When I explained it to them, I'd say something like, "Oh, I bought this great statue. It was expensive, but I got it for 50 percent off. It's so beautiful . . . I mean it has two cracks in the leg, but I enjoy it and really like it." It's almost as if I was looking for approval, or waiting to hear someone tell me I shouldn't have bought something that was already broken.

During one conversation with my mother-in-law about the statue, I of course mentioned the cracks in it, and she said something that changed my perspective completely. Her response when I explained how it was cracked was, "That's great. It makes it more human." I contemplated for a while what she had told me. What a great lesson this was for me. There I was, teaching people about impermanence, continuously explaining how things fall apart, and also promoting how to be with themselves and their lives just as they were, yet I was being driven by my own fears and insecurities over something as simple as a crack in a wooden statue. How could I accept myself and all of my "cracks" if I couldn't accept the Buddha statue with all of its flaws? How was I supposed to let go of my body and mind, and ultimately my life, if I couldn't accept that a small wooden statue could fall apart at any moment?

There will always be cracks in our lives and ourselves, and ultimately it will all fall apart. We don't have to try to immediately fill up the cracks, gluing everything back together. Instead, we can learn to accept the cracks and allow things to fall apart, letting them just be as they are, and finding ways to rejoice in their presence.

For the rest of today, find joy in all the imperfections life offers, inside and out.

Be like my cracked Buddha, perfectly at peace with itself—cracks and all.

A TRIP TO NICARAGUA

Meditation is running into reality.
—BHANTE GUNARATANA

AWHILE AGO, I went on a service-learning trip to Nicaragua. Our trip was to help educate ourselves about the many problems going on in the country, as well as what role America has played in them. There were many times when we experienced the horrors of extreme poverty and heard many stories of immense suffering. We also planned homestays with families living deep in the Nicaraguan jungles, and we visited others who literally lived in the country's largest garbage dumpsite. It was quite the eye-opener, to say the least.

Although we met with many people who were living under such harsh conditions, I was unable

to believe how joyful, peaceful, compassionate, and kind all of them were to us. They didn't
know who we were, yet they gladly embraced us
and allowed us to stay in their homes. They fed
us delicious home-cooked meals and offered all
they had to make us feel comfortable and welcome. They treated us as if we were family, or at
the very least longtime friends. Being around
them, one would never suspect they had suffered
so much, or that they lived in such conditions.
They all radiated such love and compassion with
their laughter, smiles, and genuineness.

Many of us believe our happiness depends on
external conditions being a certain way—mainly
our way. Yet experiencing these people in these
impoverished conditions proved to me that peace
and joy have nothing to do with having material things or perfect living conditions. Clearly, it
doesn't matter what kind of situation we find ourselves in; peace and joy are always possible.

True peace and joy are beyond the conditions
of our lives, and in meditation we dive directly
into these depths of our being. No matter what
we may be experiencing as we sit on our cushions, we are learning to connect with something

A TRIP TO NICARAGUA ■ 127

beyond our experience—something that holds our experience just like the sky holds the clouds.

I've had people ask me how it's possible to find peace when they're experiencing chronic pain, addicted to drugs, aging, dying, or just simply having life go differently than they had hoped. The answer lies in learning to let go of our expectations and shedding the constant need to have all we desire, all the time. Instead, we can practice contentment by letting whatever experiences we have be the way they are, all the while practicing kindness and compassion for all we encounter.

This is the path to true peace and joy—and it's not dependent on anything.

BREATHING: THE ANCHOR FOR YOUR MIND

Feelings come and go like clouds in a windy sky. Conscious breathing is my anchor.

—THICH NHAT HANH

ONE OF THE PRIMARY methods we are taught when we first begin meditating is to watch our breath. Put simply, this means to observe and stay with the sensations of each breath. The focus can be at the tips of the nostrils or on the rising and falling of the belly—whichever is easiest to focus on. Our breath becomes the anchor into the present moment—an anchor protecting us from being swept away by the fierce ocean of wandering thoughts.

Normally, wandering thoughts push and pull us all over the place. For example, we may remember hurtful words someone once said to us, and immediately we become lost in a storm of rage. Or we may reminisce about a time when things may have been happier, and soon we begin drowning in sadness and yearning. During meditation, though, we are able to see a wandering thought as just that—a wandering thought—and let it go, returning to the anchor and coming back to the breath. Without the anchor we would be endlessly tossed around at the mercy of the wandering thoughts of an untamed mind. Our breath allows us to see our mind when it moves, giving us the freedom to follow our thoughts, or simply let them go and come back to watching the breath. With practice we get to know our mind and learn which thoughts to follow and which to let go. If we can stay with this anchor all day, we will see every movement of the mind clearly and can use our own discernment to act skillfully, rather than habitually in each moment.

Throw the anchor overboard and practice staying with the breath—on the cushion in meditation, and more important, off the cushion in daily life.

Wake up and become free from unnecessary suffering.

Be vigilant.

Stay awake.

FIVE-DAY
WESTERN ZEN
RETREAT

*What a liberation to realize that the
"voice in my head" is not who I am. Who
am I, then?*

—ECKHART TOLLE

A T ONE FIVE-DAY retreat I sat at Dharma
Drum Retreat Center, I practiced intensively
with the question, "Who am I?" This short saying
became my mantra for five full days. Over and
over again, both on and off my cushion, I had to
repeat this question to myself and observe the
answers that arose in my mind. Of course, all the
answers my head produced didn't quite hit the
mark, and when I tried telling my teacher what I
thought was right, he always rejected it. Instead
of trying to solve the question, I was instructed to

rest in not knowing and tried to relax fully into the questioning itself.

Although it was a silent retreat, we did have time for private interviews with the teacher, and also did communication exercises, which were unique to this retreat. Like most retreatants here, I seemed to be very concerned with myself and my "problems." My mind was racing about the things going wrong with my life, and all my stresses and anxieties seemed, to me at least, to be *exactly* who I was. Thoughts about my problems from daily life filled my mind, swirling around emotional storms and internal chaos. It wasn't relaxing, but I continued to let go of the thoughts, judgments, feelings, and storylines, and unceasingly kept turning my attention to the question, "Who am I?"

The communication exercise was very interesting and new to me, as I was used to not talking to other practitioners on retreats. I found it very useful, though, in helping me go deeper into answering the question of who I am. The exercise went as follows: The timekeeper would signal that it was time for the communication exercise, and silently we chose a partner. Once you locked eyes with someone you hadn't sat with yet, you moved your cushion over to them and would sit down a few feet apart, face to face. A bell would ring and the partner would say, "Mark, tell me who you are." For five whole minutes, until the timekeeper rang the bell again, we were to say whatever came into our minds, without filtering it in any way. The partner, on the other hand, was only to sit and listen, without judgment. They were not able to get involved with my answers, talk back, or interact in any way. Their practice was "just listening."

Of course, in my first few sessions, my first responses were shallow and typical: my age, occupation, and all the other basics about myself. Oddly enough, I noticed there was a nervousness and fear behind all of these responses, which I couldn't quite seem to understand. I kept exploring this feeling and continued asking the damn question, "Who am I?"

Simon Child, the teacher on this specific retreat, met with me for an interview once per day. In these interviews, I could explore the question more deeply in the presence of an experienced teacher, and bring up any difficulties I was encountering in my practice. During my first interview, my anxiety and fear increased even more. What was I so afraid of? Simon explained how I was probably afraid to be exposed, and afraid to "just be" who I truly was. It didn't make any sense to me, so I returned frustrated to the meditation hall to sit through even more excruciating hours of painful meditation.

The next day in his morning Dharma talk, Simon told us to look in places where we wouldn't usually look to find more things to "empty our barrel" of all the false answers we had been coming up with in response to the question, "Who am I?" Immediately after these instructions, I began searching and was shocked at what I found. Out of nowhere I felt intense feelings of loneliness—the most intense I've ever felt in my life. This deep sadness pierced my heart and brought tears to my eyes. I began mourning as if I had lost a dear friend. I cried so hard I had to leave the meditation hall, as I was becoming such a disturbance to the other retreatants. As I huddled in a small corner, bawling my eyes out, Simon took notice and called me in for an "emergency" interview.

With Simon's guidance, I was able to see that because of specific life events in my past, I was always "acting" in ways to be accepted. I searched for people to tell me who I was, and when no one was around, I felt deeply alone and disconnected. Without people telling me who to be, who was I really? It was scary and very intense, but after I felt all the terrifying emotions and owned my experience, it eventually passed. Oddly enough, after feeling this tremendous, horrifying energy in my whole body, I began feeling much lighter. I felt free and peaceful.

After the upheaval, it was much easier to be who I was, and I began connecting more with the people on retreat, and even the nature around the retreat center. My mind was becoming more clear, calm, and peaceful. Now, when I asked myself, "Who am I?" my mind no longer sought after intellectual answers. Instead, I sat in full awareness of who I was in the present moment. During the communication exercises, I sat with this same "not-knowing" mind, sitting in silence when it was my turn to talk. Was my silence screaming the answer to the question all along?

When I went in for my next interview, Simon asked me yet again who I was, but this time I sat quietly for a minute and finally said, "This is who I am." I know it doesn't sound like I had much of a realization, but in that moment I was free from all ideas and concepts of who I was and was simply resting in my own being. There was immense joy and peace. We both laughed, and Simon said, "Yes, exactly." and the interview ended.

A day later the retreat was over, and we had to bring the wisdom and peace from our intense practice home with us to the chaos of everyday living. I felt good and was ready to do so. I imagined that I finally knew who I was, after all.

Unfortunately, my deep peace dissipated quickly when I turned on my phone and discovered painful texts from my girlfriend at the time, explaining how she had cheated on me while I was away. Mark and all his problems instantly returned with force, but there was definitely a spaciousness allowing me to hold it in a new way.

But like all difficult experiences, it was faced, dealt with, and life changed yet again.

Now you know why I keep teaching you not to attach to the peaceful feelings of meditation . . . Just like that, in an instant, they disappear.

DON'T RESIST
THE COLD

Pain is a relatively objective, physical phenomenon; suffering is our psychological resistance to what happens. Events may create physical pain, but they do not in themselves create suffering. Resistance creates suffering. Stress happens when your mind resists what is . . . The only problem in your life is your mind's resistance to life as it unfolds.

—DAN MILLMAN

I ATTENDED Montclair State University, receiving my bachelor's degree in religious studies. The campus, located in Montclair, New Jersey, is situated in a mountainous area, and because of this it's always windier and much colder, especially during the frigid winter months. I remember sitting in my car dozens of times, not wanting to walk to class, as there was no way of escaping the frosty, gusty air. No matter what kind of winter outfit I wore in preparation for that brutal walk, the wind would always find its way up my pant leg or down my neck. What made this even worse was that I hated feeling cold.

One brisk winter night, I decided to try to apply what I had learned in meditation to the cold. For that one time only, I would relax my body rather than tense it up when I walked to my car from class. I told myself that no matter what, I would observe what the cold actually feels like and see what happens. So I walked outside and was immediately hit with the stabbing, cold air. Instantly I developed goosebumps all over my body and felt that familiar sting of the moun-tainous winter air. I felt my shoulders start to tense—but this time I quickly relaxed them. When my fists started to clench, I let them go. I opened up fully to feeling very, very uncomfort-able, and I just walked and breathed, continuing to relax every time I felt the tension creeping back in. I was able to temporarily let go of the judging mind that hated being cold, and I real-ized it really wasn't that big a deal when I just faced the feelings of being cold. Sure, it was absolutely uncomfortable, but before I knew it I was in my car with my seat warmers on and the heat blowing full blast. I was back to feeling comfortable and warm again. The discomfort of being cold was over.

We can apply this simple method of relaxing into discomfort to any difficulty we encounter in our lives. For example, if we're angry with someone, just sit with the actual experience of it. It will eventually cool off and will ultimately go away.

Does it make it any less uncomfortable? No—absolutely not. But we can sit with it, be with it, and get to know it intimately.

It is not necessary to resist it or act out because of it. We don't have to give it our body or our speech.

One of the biggest things preventing us from peace is simply resistance to what is.

For just today, try letting go of the resistance to one thing that normally is perceived as a bother. Whether it be an emotion, a thought pattern, a difficult person, a difficult job, or bodily pain, try to experience it directly.

Don't fight it.

Let it come in.

Relax into it, and realize that it can be faced and that it surely will pass.

We don't need to create strategies to escape it or suppress it, but rather can transform it through allowing it to be what it is.

QUIETING
THE MIND

*When you are practicing zazen, do not
try to stop your thinking. Let it stop by
itself. If something comes into your mind,
let it come in, and let it go out. It will
not stay long. When you try to stop your
thinking, it means you are bothered by it.
Do not be bothered by anything . . . if you
are not bothered by the waves, gradually
they will become calmer and calmer.*

— SHUNRYU SUZUKI

THERE WAS A woman who used to come every
once in a while to a beginner's yoga class I
taught. One day after class she came up to me and
said, "You're always telling me to quiet my mind
and be here with my practice, but I simply can't
do it. The entire class my mind is busy planning,

remembering conversations, or simply daydreaming about nonsense. No matter how much I try, my mind is always moving and never quiet." She was very upset and frustrated and thought that yoga might not be for her. I explained to her how quieting her mind didn't mean she wouldn't have any thoughts. It just meant she could notice her thoughts instead of following or getting caught in them. I let her know how judging her mind for thinking was, in fact, adding more thoughts. To counteract her continuing to be upset with how much her mind was moving, I clarified that quieting her mind actually meant quieting her attachments to the thinking itself. For the next class I instructed her to simply allow her mind to move, rather than getting upset and struggling with its restlessness. I gave her permission to think rather than resist her monkey mind, and I made it clear to her that she could simply notice when her mind wandered off and then gently bring it back.

The next time she came in, she explained how she had told her mind it was all right to think. If her mind wanted to go off somewhere, she was going to let it. To her surprise, when she allowed her mind to be restless, it barely made a peep. Eureka. She was able to quiet her mind.

It's very important to understand that quieting your mind doesn't mean you don't think. If a teacher tells you to have no thoughts, this doesn't necessarily imply that thoughts won't arise. This may seem confusing, but it's actually quite a simple concept to understand. For example, in Zen Buddhism there is a vow that says not to let anger arise. Now obviously, if someone pisses us off, anger will naturally arise. So what is this vow pointing to? How can we not get angry when someone is pushing our buttons? Sometimes, anger just arises all on its own. How can we not let it arise if the feeling is not even in our control? The paradoxical answer lies in allowing it to arise. In fact, it's going to arise, and that's completely natural. The practice of not letting anger arise actually happens when it arises and we don't grab hold of it. We don't let it become anything more than what it is: a passing energy. By not grasping in this way, we don't become an angry person, hence anger doesn't arise. If there is no one there to own the anger, it doesn't truly arise.

So please remember, if we're practicing meditation and our mind is all over the place, that's totally fine. Everybody's mind is this way. We're not screwed up or doing something wrong.

Meditation is still for us. The power of the practice comes not from ridding our mind of thoughts, but rather from learning to sit with the madness in our head, letting go of thoughts and starting over again and again. If we find ourselves lost in a thought, we can simply wake up. Come back to the present moment and start over again. If we get lost in thought another time, wake up again. This is our practice—it has nothing to do with becoming thoughtless.

Remember, the focus is on the present moment, and yes, thoughts will try to pull us away, and as soon as we realize this has happened, we can gently come back. We can experience our thoughts as we would experience external sounds. The sounds come, and then they go. We don't have to think about or label them because as soon as we start thinking about it, the sound has already changed or gone.

Try to have this relaxed approach to the thinking mind. You don't have to get involved with your thoughts, but you also don't have to suppress them or try to forcefully stop them either. Let them come and go on their own.

You may be surprised what happens when you do.

DON'T WORRY, IT CANNOT LAST

*Impermanence is a principle of harmony.
When we don't struggle against it, we are
in harmony with reality.*

—PEMA CHÖDRÖN

THERE'S SOMETHING so powerful and profound about sitting with our problems in meditation. Let me explain a recent situation where my meditation practice helped out immensely.

The other day I was really angry with a close friend of mine after catching him in a series of lies. Initially I wanted to call him and flip out, but obviously my practice has taught me to know a little better than that. I decided instead to do an hour-long meditation, holding my anger with compassionate awareness. Unsurprisingly, it felt terrible, and I didn't want to sit there. Honestly, I almost got up after thirty seconds, but I stuck with it and watched my mind create all kinds of possible scenarios between my friend and I, along with justifications for how I felt. I observed all this coming and going, and after the first thirty minutes or so passed by, the thoughts slowly started becoming less and less. The feeling of the anger itself was also less intense, and by the end of the hour I wasn't even the slightest bit upset. I felt quite tranquil and relaxed, actually. I could still clearly see the situation wasn't right on his part, and the issue still needed to be addressed, but I was seeing clearly and was no longer caught in my anger. From that open space I wrote an email that was direct and honest, without aggression or blame.

What we start to find as we practice meditation is that everything has to pass. Anything that arises has to cease on its own. No matter how difficult an emotion, state of mind, or pain is, it has to change. It's like a flowing river. If we let it flow, it will pass. Ajahn Chah would always tell his students who would complain about their difficulties to try and maintain them. He'd tell them to set a timer for an hour or two and see how long they could keep the emotional charge. What he was trying to teach them is what I experienced firsthand. When I tried to maintain it, my anger had to change. I couldn't stay angry forever, even if I wanted to.

It's helpful to remember this, especially when in a difficult situation or when experiencing a difficult emotion. Just experience it. That's it. It's what the Buddha called the Middle Way; we're not suppressing it nor are we acting on it. We're just fully feeling it, letting it express itself and pass through. So when it comes to difficulties and suffering, don't worry—it cannot last.

THE BATHROOM
DOOR OF
THE MIND

There are many lanes on the highway of enlightenment.

—LAMA SURYA DAS

A COMMUNITY OF practitioners that follows the Buddhist path is called a *sangha*. Being part of a sangha is a great way to deepen our practice and share our experiences with like-minded spiritual friends. The particular sangha I sit with is called Heart Circle Sangha and is located at our teacher's house in Ridgewood, New Jersey. Although we meet at our teacher's house, we still use the technical Zen term of *zendo*, which means "meditation hall." Together, all of us gather for weekly meetings, which consist of silent meditations, personal one-on-one interviews with our teacher, and on certain days, dharma talks and group sharing.

Every week I have the compulsive habit of going to the bathroom right when I arrive, because our meditation practice lasts about two hours. How can I have an empty mind with a full bladder? Anyway, her bathroom has a pocket door. For those of you who don't know what that is (I just learned the name of it myself, for the sake of this book) it's a sliding door that has no handle on it. Instead, it has a little switch that, when turned, releases a hook that grabs another piece on the inside of the doorframe, keeping the door from being opened by some poor old chap. For the longest time, I could never figure out how to get this door to lock and stay shut. I'd always close it but would never know if it was truly locked or not. This made me nervous and gave me stage fright, making my pre-meditation bathroom ritual longer than planned as I fearfully peered over my shoulder, hoping no one would walk in on me.

For a while, I really couldn't stand that door. It just didn't make any sense to me. When I would close it gently, it never closed enough to lock and would be open a crack, and when I tried pressing hard against the doorframe, it still never caught correctly. Recently, though, I learned how to master that damn lock. All I had to do was close it until the door touched the frame, and then gently turn the switch. It was so simple, yet for a few bathroom trips it seemed so complex. My attempts at being too gentle and not closing the door enough or being too forceful didn't work out very well. Only when I took that middle way—not too hard, not too easy—did I get the door shut and locked. Finally, I was able to relax while in the bathroom.

There's an important message in this little story, and it's the message of how much effort we need to put into our meditation practice. Obviously in meditation, we don't want to be mindlessly sitting around doing nothing. That would be one end of the spectrum. At the same time, we also don't want to be too militaristic about it, aggressively trying to kill off all thoughts. It's important to find a balance between the two. Are we too relaxed, so that we're drifting off and spacing out? Or are we trying too hard, forcing our mind to be something that it's not in that moment? The answer will always be different. Sometimes we may be too relaxed and will need to wake ourselves up a bit by opening our eyes or fixing our posture. Other times we may find ourselves straining too much and will have to let go of the effort and just rest in what is.

Try to find the middle way between the two extremes of too gentle and too aggressive. It's up to you to find the way to lock the bathroom door of your mind.

ASKING LIFE WHAT IT CANNOT GIVE US

Our attempts to find lasting pleasure, lasting security, are at odds with the fact that we're part of a dynamic system in which everything and everyone is in process.

—PEMA CHÖDRÖN

A LOT OF OUR suffering comes from asking life for what it cannot ever give us. I have found that there are three main things that we tend to ask for, all of which life simply can't deliver. The first thing we ask for is permanence. We want things to forever be the way they are. We work hard to get our life situations and ourselves the way we want, and we would like them to stay that way. Although on some level we clearly know that change is inevitable, we somehow delude ourselves into believing that it's going to be some other way.

Impermanence is probably one of the most important teachings. In Buddhist thought it's *the* teaching, and if we can truly understand it on a very deep level, we'll find a great amount of peace in our lives. Once we find a way to dance with impermanence rather than fight with it, we will feel much better. This is much easier said than done because our minds are programmed to believe in permanence.

Another thing we ask of life that it just cannot give us is to be comfortable all the time. We truly believe that we are supposed to be cozy and happy every day, but this is clearly not the case, as there's aging, sickness, and ultimately death, leaving everything and everyone we love behind. No matter how hard we try to avoid discomfort and pain, we ultimately have to encounter unpleasant people, situations, and feelings. With that said, it's not all going to be bad, but eventually we are going to have to face the fact that many times throughout our lives we will experience mild to extreme discomfort. Instead of desperately trying to maintain pleasure, happiness, and comfort—which goes back to the false belief in permanence again—and instead of trying to avoid discomfort at all costs, we can learn to embrace both comfort and discomfort equally. This is what we train in when we meditate. We sit without distractions and open up to whatever arises in that moment, whether we like what we are experiencing or not.

The last big thing we ask life for is security. We would like to know that we're safe and secure. Clearly, because of the truth of impermanence, no situation is ever free from uncertainty and insecurity, but this still doesn't stop us from desperately wanting security. Actually, if we look at how our society is set up, we will find that it is based on this false belief of security. We have houses so we don't have to worry about where we will have to sleep. Having our own place makes us feel safe and secure. We also have grocery stores so we never have to worry about where we're going to get our next meal. We feel secure knowing that if we go to the store, food will be there waiting for us. This is much better than our ancestors had it, with them not knowing where or what their next meal would be. It all comes down to feeling secure in an uncertain, chaotic world.

These ideas of permanence, eternal happiness, and security are not only prominent outside of ourselves, but even more so on the inside. Our small-mindedness gives us the illusion of safety and permanence. Identifying with them keeps us stuck with our habitual tendencies, beliefs, and storylines, making us feel secure and safe in this uncertain world. At least when we wake up in the morning, we know for sure that we will react a certain way throughout our day. This brings us a great sense of security and familiarity, keeping us from facing the constant uncertainty and impermanence of the reality of our lives. We may find in our meditation practice that's it's hard and scary to let go of our self-centered, egoistic tendencies, simply because of this deep yearning for security and permanence.

Learning to relax into uncertainty, impermanence, and discomfort is probably the last thing we ever want to do. Paradoxically, the more we can practice with them as they happen in our lives, the more peace we will actually experience. As we become better at facing situations that bring us face to face with these facts of life, we become less afraid of them and can finally relax into the ambiguity of our lives.

If at any point today any of these false beliefs are experienced, try facing the feelings and thoughts that arise with them. Let go of the story-lines about it and relax into whatever is left. With an open heart, confront the feelings of ground-lessness or anxiety that may come up. Right there, amid the fear and discomfort true trans-formation is possible.

Please be sure not to ask life what it cannot ultimately deliver.

EVERYTHING
THAT ARISES
PASSES AWAY

All conditioned things are impermanent—
when one sees this with wisdom, one turns
away from suffering.

—BUDDHA

I WAS recently reading a book by Toni Bernhard, *How to Wake Up*, when I came across a line I have heard many times before from my own teachers: *Everything that arises passes away.* As simple and obvious as this statement is, these five words contain an enormous amount of depth and wisdom. Everything I try to teach and convey through my articles, talks, meditation retreats, and yoga classes can be found in this one short sentence. Whether it's thoughts, feelings, sensations, sounds, plants, animals, people, or planets, everything that arises passes away. If one were able to truly understand the depth of this message, they would be fully and completely liberated from all their suffering.

Suffering comes in many forms, but the unnecessary suffering in life basically comes down to two things: aversion and attachment—not wanting what we have and not having what we want. Put another way, we always tend to feel that something is wrong or missing. For example, we want more money but don't have it, or we have anxiety and don't want it.

Everything that arises passes away. How can this one sentence possibly save someone from suffering in these examples? Money will come and money will go. We have all heard of people who were completely loaded but quickly lost everything. Even someone who is filthy rich and only getting richer will eventually have to pass away, ultimately losing everything. What will their money do for them then? Nothing, except maybe pay for their funeral. Even the desire itself for more money is just something that arises and ceases—a thought that could either be attached to and suffered over, or simply noticed and released. Obviously I'm not advocating not caring about money at all, or that we don't need to work hard to make it, but my message is to know that no matter what our circumstances may currently be, they will ultimately change. "Gain" arises and passes away, as does "loss." We must learn to welcome and relax into both if we want to be truly at ease with our life.

In the case of anxiety, there is also some good news here. Anxiety arises, which means that it has to pass away. When we experience anxiety, it may seem like it will never go away, or that it never changes, but if we pay close enough attention, we will find the feeling itself is constantly changing in intensity. We can begin to notice moments in the day where we are not anxious, like when we're laughing with a friend or taking a nice big bite out of a hot fudge sundae (What? Just me?).

By bringing mindfulness into our day, we can notice how all that arises passes away. Dreams end upon waking, lying down changes into standing up, full bladder passes away to empty bladder, etc. Our whole day is full of thoughts, sensations, situations, and people arising and ceasing. If we recognize this fact, we won't become so stuck on having life go according to our terms, nor will we be lost in grasping on to pleasurable experiences or feelings, while desperately trying to escape unpleasant ones. All of this arises and passes away anyway. Why not, instead, train our hearts and minds to be spacious enough to include all of it? This is our path and our practice.

Pay attention and relax. It will all pass away. Fully embrace life right now because this too shall pass.

Everything that arises passes away.

UNDERSTANDING
BUDDHIST
MEDITATION

Sit down, shut up, watch, and don't get involved. Gradually, the meditation experience will open up all by itself.

—AJAHN BRAHM

IN THE BUDDHIST tradition, meditation is used as a way to cultivate loving-kindness, compassion, and wisdom—not only for ourselves but for all sentient beings. It's a tool that's used for liberation from the suffering of life, the suffering of aging, sickness, and death. Meditation cultivates clear awareness of the present moment—mindfulness. It is only in the present moment where we can find peace and freedom from that which shackles us.

The present moment is full of an ever-changing array of feelings, sounds, thoughts, perceptions, smells, tastes, and sensations. When we further investigate these phenomena, we find they all have a transitory nature. Nothing ever stays the same, and because of this we learn that nothing can enduringly fulfill us or be permanently grasped. These realizations lead to wisdom, or the understanding that all things in the universe are interrelated. There is no solid, separate self alone in a cold universe, but rather one ever-changing present moment of interaction and change. According to Buddhism, directly experiencing this truth is liberation.

Some traditions or modern new age beliefs suggest that meditation is a way of gaining material things: wealth, happiness, all which we may desire—and all of which have some self-centered idea of gaining something for ourselves. From the Buddhist perspective, self-centered thinking is what we are learning to let go of, as this is the main cause of suffering in our lives. It's important not to confuse letting go of self-centered thinking as having no preferences at all in this lifetime. Practice is not meant to make us become a rock sitting at the bottom of a lake, cold and lifeless.

Preferences are encouraged. There is nothing wrong with preferring life or people to be a certain way; this is not the problem. Our attachment to these preferences, making them into requirements, creates suffering.

In Buddhist meditation, we follow the breath, staying open to the present moment, rather than shutting everything else out and solely focusing on a single point. The single point of focus is the entire present moment without grasping, attachment, or aversion. Things are simply left as they are. Buddhists refer to this as "suchness" or "isness"—the one ever-changing present moment, complete in itself, interacting and changing. It's only the mind that separates this one moment into self and other, or self and environment.

Through meditation the mind quiets and the veils of separation slowly dissolve. We are left to rest in our completeness and wholeness in the present moment—no self, no problems.

Many believe meditation is a way to become better or fixed. While it's true that the fruits of meditation may make a "better" person, the true purpose of practice has no such ideas of perfection. The concept of perfection comes from the self-centered thought that there is something wrong with the present moment and that it needs to be fixed or made better. This kind of thinking keeps us constantly seeking out new experiences outside of the present moment. When this happens, true peace will never be an option. If we can't live peacefully in this moment, we can't live peacefully anywhere. Craving to change or control the present moment is what we are learning to release in order to find the freedom we have been searching for all along.

The good news is that it's not far away. Meditation allows us to be who we are, each and every moment. Its power comes not from forcing change or trying to attain something, but in the simple ability to let things be as they are. Each moment is enlightenment if we can learn to continuously rest in the fullness of the present moment, moment after moment. This all sounds very simple, and it is, but simple doesn't necessarily mean easy. Practice never ends and will last an entire lifetime—maybe even more than one.

Start right now. There is no other time.

WHY ME?

To live is to suffer; to survive is to find some meaning in the suffering.
—FRIEDRICH NIETZSCHE

MANY OF US have asked or heard someone say, "Why is this happening to me?" It's a common question when facing any of life's painful or confusing moments, and it often brings about additional suffering to that which is already difficult. But have we ever really received a satisfactory answer to this question? Even if we did, did it actually bring the peace we were seeking?

Perhaps we could ask a different question: "Why not me?" This opens things up and reminds us that we are not above the basic truths of life. It's true; we can be a good person and still get cancer. We can do virtuous deeds and still die in a pointless accident, or suffer some unimagined tragedy.

Suffering and difficulty happen to all of us. It's simply the fact of our existence. "Why not me?" acknowledges this truth and allows us to become a willing, engaged participant in whatever may be occurring. When we aren't busy resisting what's happening and trying to figure out the *why*, we can get into the *how* and begin finding ways to manage living with this new experience.

Rather than asking, "Why is this happening to me?" we could instead ask, "Why is this happening for me?" This allows us to see this difficulty as our path to awakening. What is our practice during these times? What can be learned or cultivated? Now, you may be wondering, how can a cancer diagnosis, the loss of a loved one, or other forms of suffering we may face be teaching me anything? Well, it is through our suffering that we are able to get in touch with the tenderness underneath the rigid walls of our small-minded ego. It is our suffering that allows us to experience compassion for the suffering of others, and reminds us of the preciousness of this life we are living. It puts us face to face with who we are and reminds us of our deepest values and what is truly important. The truth is, every difficult situation life presents us with is a chance to see who we really are. The more life breaks us down, the more we get in touch with that which is indestructible. When tragedy strikes, we lose security and become groundless. This may be one of the scariest times we ever experience, yet it can also be one of the most profound if we are able to pay attention to it.

Instead of getting lost in the endless questioning of "Why me?" try turning toward it and learn how to be with the physical experience of emotions during this time. Without adding the extra storylines and judgments, simply rest in the discomfort and groundlessness. Get to know it. Make friends with it. Feel the emotions brought out by this event for what they are: passing, uncomfortable energy. Like a cloud in the sky, our emotions and thoughts are just moving through our mind, and as quickly as they came they will soon vanish without a trace. If we label these thoughts and emotions as our own and believe the clouds to be the sky, we'll quickly attach ourselves to them and keep them around longer. It's as if we're reliving the same nightmare over and over again. And if we think we can just run away from them and hide, we'll be in for a big surprise. As Bob Marley put it so well, "You can't run away from yourself." The emotions will hide and build up more and more until the moment they feel necessary to release, and then we will have to deal with even more than we bargained for.

Stop wasting time with "Why me?" Try asking yourself, "Why not me?" Or even, "Why is this happening for me?" Change your perspective on what's happening. Allow yourself to be vulnerable and let this difficult time soften your being. Be kind in this moment and bring yourself the compassion you need. Even *this* experience can be used as a way to awaken yourself.

FERTILIZER

When shit happens, turn it into fertilizer.
—KUTE BLACKSON

AT THE BEGINNING of spring my father begins cultivating and preparing his garden in order to produce fresh herbs and vegetables. His garden is full of basil, mint, tomatoes, eggplant, and much more. Apart from turning the soil and planting the seeds, my father also puts fertilizer down so his garden will blossom. Fertilizer gives his garden the essential nutrients necessary for optimal growth among the plants. Although there are many manmade chemical fertilizers on the market, classic fertilizer is made with manure—leading to the time-honored practice of using shit to make plants grow to their full potential. On the one hand, it's quite disgusting to think about, yet this process is profound and can teach us a lot about the "shit" in our lives.

Imagine our struggles, difficulties, neuroses, and bad habits as manure that nourishes the garden of our meditation practice. Instead of trying to remove these parts of our lives, we can actually use them as a way to cultivate the qualities of wisdom, compassion, and kindness. We can embrace our difficulties in a new way so they can nourish us rather than bring us down.

This method of fertilization truly portrays the path we are following as serious meditators. Nothing is left out; everything is included—absolutely everything. From the most terrifying moments in our lives to the most beautiful ones, every single part is used as a way to deepen our practice. In this way, everything becomes our teacher. We may start out believing that these difficulties are blocking us from our path, but, as mentioned before, actually accepting and working with these very struggles *is* our path. We can either fight the problems we experience, separating the sacred and mundane, or we can use them as fertilizer to cultivate the good qualities that we produce in the process of cultivating.

The next time a difficulty arises we can use it as an alert to practice. In that moment, we can allow it to become the fertilizer for our spiritual garden. During these times we can pay attention and see what thoughts we are thinking and believing. We then can discover the physical sensations this difficulty is creating, and find out how and where we feel it. Is it fiery? Empty? Throbbing? Remember, seeing clearly is wisdom in and of itself. It's the beginning of learning how our mind creates suffering. Resting with the sensations and thoughts, without judgments or labels, will also cultivate kindness and compassion. Don't forget, we can do this with anything: getting ill, being around someone who's not doing well or whom we know is dying, anxiety, depression, pain . . . Use it all to cultivate this path.

It's possible to use all the "shit" of our lives to fertilize a beautiful garden of compassion and wisdom.

Get to it.

MOTIVATION FROM DIFFICULTIES

*In your very imperfections you will find
the basis for your firm, Way-seeking mind.*
—Suzuki Roshi

IN THE LAST CHAPTER, I talked about using our difficulties, our bad behaviors, or our bad habits as a fertilizer to cultivate compassion, wisdom, and kindness. Now I'd like to expand on this and use these same difficulties as motivation to continue with our meditation practice.

Suzuki Roshi once talked about four kinds of horses: excellent ones, good ones, poor ones, and bad ones. He explained how the excellent horse would run before it saw the shadow of the whip, the good horse would run right before the whip hit its skin, the poor horse would run only when it felt the pain of the whip on its body, and the bad horse would run only when the pain penetrated the marrow of its bones. When people hear this, they immediately want to be the best horse, but Suzuki Roshi explained that when learning comes too easily, it actually keeps us from working hard. When it comes to meditation, many believe they should be the best horse, so to speak—the one that can sit and have no problems, easily relaxing into it without any struggles.

But as Suzuki clarified, the worst horse is the best to be.

When we struggle, whether in meditation or in life, it's actually better for our practice. Having more problems in practice and in our lives motivates us to seek something beyond them. When everything is fine and dandy, why would we want to look deeply at anything? Why would we want to question our suffering if we aren't suffering at all? Why would we want to liberate ourselves from our struggles if there were none present? We must look at the difficulties in our lives not as something we need to conquer or get rid of but as blessings in disguise—heavenly messengers telling us to go deeper.

Suzuki Roshi also talked about the same analogy, but with a parent, explaining how people who think they are the best parents probably never are. Since they already think they're great, there won't be the same level of effort exerted as someone who thinks they are the worst parent. These parents are constantly putting great effort in. We cannot misunderstand this, though, and take it the wrong way. We don't need to intentionally think of ourselves in a negative way, or constantly put ourselves down in order to have a good meditation practice.

When we struggle in meditation or daily life, we don't need to fight it. Instead, we can use it as motivation to go beyond it and find something more solid—something deeper within ourselves that we can depend on. The only way out of our suffering is diving right into it—going through it, experiencing it. I am well aware this may be the last thing we want to do, but we must try.

We can try to see the difficulties we are experiencing right now as not necessarily negative things—almost like blessings in disguise. We can use them as motivation to continue our meditative journey into the depths of our being.

Let us all learn, explore, and find freedom right in the midst of the chaos.

THE SPIDER
OR THE FLY?

*Do not get caught in your anger, worries, or
fears. Come back to the present moment,
and touch life deeply. This is mindfulness.*
—THICH NHAT HANH

IN MEDITATION PRACTICE, we try our best to not
get caught in anything, whether it's a sound,
thought, or feeling. I always say practice makes
us like a spider. Think about it. A spider creates
an intricate, sticky web, yet it somehow effortlessly walks across it, never once getting stuck or
caught in it. Imagine our own sense of self—the
thoughts, storylines, emotions, body sensations,
beliefs, judgments, and expectations (all the
things that make up who we think we are) as our
very own complex web. It is a *very* sticky web, and
it is easy to get caught.

Before we practice meditation, it's as if we are a fly trying to cross the web. And a fly is not much like a spider at all. The fly takes one step into the web and its leg immediately gets stuck. It takes another step and its other leg gets stuck. Then it tries to use another leg to get those legs out, and now all its legs are stuck. The fly begins to panic and starts fighting and struggling, and before it knows what's going on, it's completely tangled in the web.

This is actually how most of us live our daily lives. We have a thought. We get stuck on the thought. We believe it and are immediately caught. We have an emotion. We stick to the emotion. We actually believe this emotion is who we are, and we begin acting it out or speaking from it. Or we may even try to do something in order to get rid of it as soon as possible. The same thing happens with bodily pain and discomfort. It arises and we are instantly stuck. "This is my pain and I don't like it."

Meditation offers us a new way to be with our lives and ourselves, and it allows us to be just like the spider walking effortlessly across its web. With practice we learn to sit and observe our own unique web of thoughts and emotions, and we practice getting unstuck. It is fully possible to exist with our emotions, thoughts, and habits—especially the bad ones—in a way where we don't get caught in them so often.

Just don't expect to shift instantly from the fly to the spider. Honestly, I don't believe we ever fully become the spider, but there will definitely be more and more days when we are less stuck. There may also be times when we realize we're stuck, and instead of freaking out like the fly and getting ever more tangled in our webs, we will gently free ourselves. All it takes is some mindfulness and awareness, and willingly showing up every day for the simple practice of meditation. Sitting in meditation we become spider-like. We are no longer caught in the complex web of our minds.

So who will we be: the spider or the fly?

INTERNAL WEATHER

Emotions are like passing storms, and you have to remind yourself that it won't rain forever.

—AMY POEHLER

A S THE SEASONS CHANGE so does the weather, as we all know.

In the fall (at least where I live) we have hurricanes, thunderstorms, and cooler air. With the winter maybe we get snow, sleet, and freezing rain. Spring brings showers and new life, and the summer brings sizzling heat. Regardless of what the weather is outside, we still have to wake up every day and get on with our lives—whether we like it or not. Some days upon waking there's a foot of snow, and we must shovel our way out of our house. On these cold, snowy days, we have to wear certain types of clothing to protect us from the cold air. Other days are wet and full of rain, calling for an umbrella and some rain boots. Still, other days are scorching hot, so we carry around water and wear less clothing to keep cool.

The truth is, we have no control over what the weather does, but regardless of this lack of control, we humans have found ways to survive. Umbrellas, gloves, boots, shorts, and so on are all a variety of the attire we've invented as a species for each specific type of weather condition we may face throughout our lives. In the same way, our inner world of thoughts and emotions is just as unpredictable and beyond our control. Some days we wake up sad and are not really sure why. Or a friend may say something that immediately triggers anxiety and unease. Sometimes just seeing someone we don't like floods our being with uncomfortable emotions, memories, and thoughts. I've never known anyone who woke up saying, "I can't wait for my mind to obsess over this all day," or "Looking forward to being depressed tomorrow!" We usually just wake up and there it is, an uninvited guest arrives in our being.

Meditation gives us tools that allow us to pay more attention to our internal weather—to the movement of our minds and our emotional worlds. We begin realizing that those thoughts and emotions aren't necessarily always things we choose or want to be thinking or feeling. Instead, much like the weather, they are just conditions reacting to other conditions, at times creating intense storms.

Meditation also teaches us to see the impermanent nature of our thoughts and emotions. Maybe we felt anxious in the morning, but after a few hours it changes. We might have been furious yesterday at a situation, yet today it's no big deal. I can remember plenty of times when I was completely heated at a situation, only to laugh the following day at how silly it was.

If we can think of our inner world (our inner weather) as no different from our outer world (the outer weather), we will see how useless it is to make a big deal out of our depression, anger, grief, or any difficult emotions or states of mind. Instead of struggling with our internal weather, we can just prepare ourselves for the storm, gear up, and get through our day. It really is no different from preparing for a snowstorm. No matter how much we complain about how it's snowing, we still have to get on our snow outfit and shovel ourselves out in order to make it to work on time.

What steps must we take to prepare for our internal weather?

First we must realize these passing storms are not who we are.

Next we should acknowledge their impermanent nature. Just like a spring shower, it cannot last.

Finally we must have the courage to let it flow through us as storms freely flow through the sky without affecting it. We must be willing to feel the ouch of our lives.

This is a very real possibility for all of us—but we must continue to practice.

LIVING BEYOND CULTURAL CONDITIONING

Being considered crazy by those who are still victims of cultural conditioning is a compliment.

—Jason Hairston

THE CULTURE or cultures we grow up in play large roles in our identity and condition our behavior and the way we view the world—but sometimes our cultural conditioning can create blind spots.

As a practicing meditator and a citizen of American culture, I have explored and discovered much cultural conditioning in myself that actually prevents, dare I say, success in meditation. These learned ways of experiencing myself and the world around me often kept me blind to the simplicity of the practice. When teaching students of mine how to begin a meditation practice, I often see in them these same conditionings I've found in myself.

The cultural condition I see most often is people believing they have no time to meditate. They'll tell me they are too busy and don't want to waste any time sitting still and doing nothing. They act as if life has them enslaved and they have no choice but to be constantly busy. This specific conditioning is also heavily mixed with the idea that if we are doing nothing, someone else is going to get ahead of us. We have been programmed to think of the world only through a competitive, business approach. We may think that someone else is doing something to get further ahead of us in life while we are sitting there meditating. It's important to remember that we are in control of our schedules. If there were an emergency and someone we love were in the hospital, wouldn't we make time? It all comes down to our priorities and time management. If we want to meditate five minutes a day, all we need to do is wake up five minutes earlier, or go to bed five minutes later. You can even go sit on the toilet at work for five minutes every day. No one will bother you there (although they may think you're having some gastrointestinal issues).

Lack of time and our competitiveness are not the only cultural conditionings harming our meditation practice. Now, more so than ever, we are a culture of distraction and instant gratification. Most of us are so used to distracting ourselves with TV, cellphones, and other forms of exciting distractions that when we begin meditating, our minds are completely bored within seconds of sitting on our cushion. The mind immediately begins searching for that next distraction. We are a country that's very good at distracting ourselves from the realities of life, and this makes it even harder to sit in meditation. With practice, though, we learn to see through our restless desires and actually find peace in "not-doing," and we find the distractions of our lives are actually keeping us from the very peace we are seeking.

A culture of instant gratification is another major problem meditation practitioners face. Our culture doesn't want to put in the work or wait for results. *We want it now, dammit!*

Take working out, for instance. As a personal trainer, I often saw people who, rather than putting in hard work and slowly getting fit over time, would instead want it right then and there. They wanted to know what pill would speed up their metabolism, or what doctor or fad diet could instantly suck the fat out of them. This approach of seeking instant results in meditation will be very disappointing, and possibly dangerous. The purpose of meditation is simply to meditate, not to get results. The joy comes from the dedication to the practice, not from getting some ecstatic state of mind, and this all takes time. If someone wants an instant spiritual experience, then LSD or mushrooms may work for them, but this is not the way of a true meditation practitioner seeking real peace.

Another problem our culture creates for meditation is that it's very ego-oriented. Everything is about the individual. Standing out in the crowd and showing off what we have seems to be the norm. Just take a peek on social media and see the narcissism. Most people are taking hundreds, if not thousands of pictures of themselves, over and over again. It's almost as if people need to remind themselves of how great they are; the more likes they get the better they feel about themselves. From a meditation point of view, focusing solely on ourselves is the biggest cause of our suffering. In fact, meditation is one of the only practices that doesn't encourage inflation of the ego. Don't get me wrong; there is nothing wicked about promoting ourselves and finding our own unique way through life, but when it becomes obsessive, and our happiness and worth become dependent on it, suffering will surely follow.

These are only a few of the cultural conditions we may find in our practice, and I bring them up not to make anyone feel bad or to say our culture is screwed up, but instead to give us something to contemplate and become curious about. We must see our conditioning deeply and repeatedly in order to see how it creates suffering in our lives and actually blocks us from experiencing a true meditation practice.

We must understand where our culture blinds us, and we must remove the veils in order to see our lives clearly and openly.

MOVIES WITH WISDOM

Nothing can harm you as much as your own thoughts unguarded.

—BUDDHA

ROWING UP, I was terrified of the movie *A Nightmare on Elm Street*. Freddy Krueger always scared me with his razor-sharp finger-knives. I vividly remember having nightmares after watching the movie in which Freddy would attack me. Although quite a frightening concept, the truth is that nightmares weren't the only thing to be found on Elm Street. In fact, much wisdom can be learned from its liberating, deeper meaning.

In the movie, Freddy Krueger was a serial killer who haunted people in their dreams. In these nightmares, he was able to hurt and even kill his frightened victims. The ones who survived would wake up to real life with gashes and wounds from his violent attacks—that is, if they were alive to wake up. Freddy would only be able to attack when they fell asleep, hence the reason the characters in the movie continued to keep themselves awake. By the end of the movie, though, protagonist Nancy Thompson finally figured out a way to destroy Freddy Krueger once and for all. She realized he could only harm her when she believed he was real. He was only a character in her dream world—he wasn't real—so when she woke up to this truth, she was finally able to rob him of all his power over her.

In our actual lives, Freddy Krueger comprises the destructive, neurotic aspects of our mind. We all have these aspects in one form or another, lurking deep within our unconscious mind, and much like Freddy, they are waiting for us to fall asleep so they can bring chaos into our lives.

The Buddha said, "No one can harm you, not even your worst enemy, as much as your own untrained mind." This statement is exactly what the ending to the movie is implying. Just as Nancy realized Freddy wasn't real and was finally able to defeat him, so too can we realize that our thoughts are no more than dreams passing through our minds. They are not as real as we'd like to believe, and only when we fall asleep by losing awareness can they bring harm to our lives. But if we can instead see our thoughts as passing dreams that cannot actually hurt us, we may find we can liberate ourselves from them.

Thanks, Wes Craven, for your profound Buddhist insight. Rest in peace.

Another great movie with wisdom is *A Beautiful Mind*, which is based on a true story about a mathematical genius named John Forbes Nash, Jr. Throughout the movie, we are introduced to important people in John's life, including his former college roommate Charles, his beloved niece Marcee, and William Parcher, a mysterious Department of Defense agent. (Please stop reading this chapter here if you've never seen this movie. There will be spoilers.) Eventually, John realizes these three are not actually real, but only figments of his imagination; John is in fact schizophrenic, and these three characters never actually existed. Upon his shocking realization, he decides to let them go, explaining to them how he knows they aren't real and how he will no longer be interacting with them.

At first they are very upset with John, and for a while they will not leave him alone, screaming and yelling at him in their attempts to interact with him, or at the very least, get his attention. But John doesn't break his vow of silence with them, and eventually they stop trying to talk to him altogether. Although they never fully disappear—we still see them in the background, walking quietly around wherever he goes—they no longer interact with him.

I have found no better movie than this to describe the long, difficult process of letting go of our attachments to our thoughts, beliefs, storylines, and emotions that make up who we think we are. In the very beginning we are totally lost in the concept of ourselves that we have created.

It all seems so real—the worries, desires, aversions, etc. The truth is, they are no more real than John's three schizophrenic hallucinations. When we first see how involved and attached we are, it is quite overwhelming. The idea of letting go of these aspects of ourselves is rather frightening, and it may seem as though we are letting go

of an old friend. Much like the movie, the beginning phases of letting go are filled with angst and
chaos. Our thoughts don't want us to disbelieve
them; our small mindedness is threatened by the
idea of liberation. Yet with time and much practice, the resistance to our freedom lessens until
we are able to see our neuroses, without becoming ensnared by them. The temptation to grab
hold of our limited, selfish views lessens, and liberation slowly but surely follows.

I'm sure there are many more movies with
just as much wisdom as the two I've chosen for
this chapter, but these are by far my favorites.
They clearly and accurately show important
teachings and aspects of undertaking a serious
meditation practice.

May we all take their wisdom and apply it.

CONTRADICTIONS IN INSTRUCTION

Now, I am like them. For the peace and comfort of living beings I use various gateways to the Dharma to proclaim the Buddha Way. Through the power of wisdom, knowing the nature and desires of living beings, I teach them the Dharma using skillful means, bringing them great joy.

—THE LOTUS SUTRA

ON THE MEDITATIVE PATH, we may sometimes encounter teachings and instructions that seem contradictory. One minute a teacher is telling us to use the object of meditation to cut off all thoughts, and the next minute they are telling us that thoughts are no big deal and to just let them be. Instances like this may happen quite often, leaving us feeling befuddled, or making it seem as if the teacher is inexperienced or doesn't know what he or she is talking about. The truth is, a good teacher will always meet their students exactly where they are. Although it may seem contradictory, there are many different ways to teach the same thing, all of which depend upon where a particular student is on their path.

Many of the disciples of meditation master Ajahn Chah were frustrated by his teachings since he would tell one person one thing and somebody else another. They often wondered which approach was the "right" approach, and they would be frustrated by the seemingly contradictory teachings. When asked about these contradictions, Ajahn Chah clarified the confusion by giving an analogy of his students walking down a curvy road. He explained how when he saw one student going off the path too far to the left, he would tell them to go right, and when he saw another student veering off to the right, he would tell them to go left. Right and left are two completely different directions, yet both are skillful means intended to keep his students walking straight on the winding road.

So when we work with a teacher we trust, or if we read books from various teachers, and the teachings they offer seem to contradict each other, remember this story and see how they are all using skillful means as a way to keep people from veering off the windy, meditative path.

THE WISDOM OF ATLANTIC CITY

Life is like stepping onto a boat which is
about to sail out to sea and sink.
—SHUNRYU SUZUKI

THIS PAST CHRISTMAS I bought my wife and myself a Groupon deal for a two-night stay at the Taj Mahal in Atlantic City. To make a long story short, we lost pretty much all the money we had brought. I had been to the Taj Mahal once before, right when I turned 21, and had lost everything—even after having won almost three hundred dollars from a twenty-dollar bill. I quickly learned from that experience that I'll most likely lose everything I bring to this enticing, money-sucking place. During this more recent venture to Atlantic City, I had brought a certain amount of money with the clear knowledge I was going to lose it all, which made leaving with nearly empty pockets not so upsetting—at least for me. Being clear about the situation, knowing I would most likely lose everything, I was able to just enjoy myself. Sometimes I was ahead, sometimes I was toward the bottom, but in the end, of course, I lost it all.

Looking back on my experience, I had what Oprah Winfrey would call an "*aha* moment." This experience is analogous to my life. No matter how much I earn, no matter what my status is in society, no matter how much my family loves me, and no matter how safe and secure I try and make myself, I am still going to lose everything. As Suzuki Roshi says, "Life is like setting sail on a ship that is bound to sink."

We will have ups and downs—sometimes feeling on top of the world, other times being crushed by its weight—but this is it. This is our life. Although this may seem like a daunting realization, it is a realization nonetheless, and is one that can bring us to peace. Once we deeply understand that we will lose everything, we realize that we've got nothing to lose and that nothing can be grasped onto. As Steve Jobs explained,

"Remembering that you are going to die is the best way I know to avoid the trap of thinking you have something to lose. You are already naked. There is no reason not to follow your heart."

Meditation and mindfulness slow us down enough to allow us to see life clearly as it is. Pleasant feelings come and go, as do unpleasant ones. Nothing can bring you ultimate fulfillment in this world; the biggest lie our minds try to make us believe is that something can. Anything that may be fulfilling now will eventually have to be let go of, or it will change. What once fulfilled us yesterday annoys us today. "If only I had this" soon becomes "If only I had that." Many times, perhaps, we have received what we have wanted, but have we ever become ultimately fulfilled? Are we finally satisfied yet? When does craving end? Unfortunately, it doesn't. The question is, how long will we continue feeding our craving before we realize this?

When we let go of wanting to fix life and realize everything will be gone before we know it, we'll finally start truly living. Each moment becomes special, and gratitude fills our heart. We will become fearless and face what life gives us.

Remember, things are simply as they are in this moment.

Peace is nothing special and it's not far away. Peace is not an attainment. We don't have to do something special to achieve it. Peace is an absence—an absence of small-mindedness, an absence of attaching to hopes and fears. It comes from becoming fully ourselves in this very moment, no matter what the circumstances, and living with open arms and an open heart.

We must try to find peace and joy right now while we're still conscious human beings. We must live our lives fully before it's too late. What are we waiting for?

We must tell people in our lives how important they are and do the things we love. Most important, we must understand we are going to lose everything, so there's literally nothing to lose. Let's understand the rules of our lives, and, just like me on my trip to the Taj Mahal, let's go play the games joyfully, knowing we are going to completely lose everything.

TURNING
INWARD
FOR TRUE
HAPPINESS

Happiness is an inside job.
—SYLVIA BOORSTEIN

IN A SOCIETY WHERE all promises of happiness are "outside" ourselves, we rarely think to turn our gaze inward. We strive to gain as many possessions as we can, but even when we have everything we ever could want, it never seems to be enough. All things in the material world fade, and so do the feelings associated with them, leaving us with familiar feelings of emptiness and a nagging anxiety for something more. We end up drowning in a sea of insatiable desires, with hopes that the next job we get, the new car we buy, or the next relationship we are in will be the answer to all our dreams and make these bad feelings disappear forever. Unfortunately this never turns out to be true because desires are endless when we're seeking satisfaction outside ourselves.

So where are we to turn for true, lasting happiness? Inward, of course. Once we are truly content and accepting of being who and where we are, our desires become less intense. The simple practice and discipline of being fully in each moment can bring great joy and peace of mind, no matter what kind of circumstances arise. We begin to realize our hearts and minds are spacious enough to hold life, no matter what flavor it may be.

We start this process of looking inward by cutting ourselves wide open and diving deep into the core of our being, finding both the things we like about ourselves and the things we don't like. Accepting both begins to create equanimity and compassion, and is the first step toward true peace and joy in our lives. By simply watching our mind and examining the emotions and reactions that come up throughout the day, we can start investigating our most deeply held beliefs, identifying the ones we are grasping tightly onto and clearly seeing how they limit our lives. We will find how some are wholesome and skillful, while others are not so much. As we become more and more familiar with the shifting belief systems in our mind, we can ask ourselves, where did these beliefs come from? Are they true? What would our lives be like if we were able to let them go? If this doesn't seem like a possibility, we can simply notice the resistance.

What's keeping us attached to these views? Are they bringing us happiness, or keeping us stuck in our suffering? Are we willing to become curious, and explore and expose our beliefs as we continue journeying deeper and deeper into who we *think* we are?

We must go inward for this to be possible.

Our happiness depends on it.

THE WONDERFUL EXPERIENCE OF A KIDNEY STONE

Learning is a gift. Even when pain is your teacher.

—MAYA WATSON

LAST JULY I went to the doctor because I felt as though I had a urinary tract infection. My bladder felt full, and going to the bathroom was slightly uncomfortable. They tested my urine and oddly enough found no infection, but since I had symptoms that mimicked a UTI, my doctor prescribed me antibiotics, just to be safe. Two days after my doctor's visit, I was sitting alone at my mother's house reading a book when all of a sudden I felt a twinge in my back. It was almost like I had tweaked a muscle, yet as soon as I stood up to stretch it out I was immediately hit with a stabbing pain that brought me face-down to the floor. The intense pain caused me to scream and made me burst into tears. There I was, all alone, in excruciating pain, and unsure of what was happening. Luckily, my phone was nearby, and I was able to text my mother, who was two blocks away at my sister's house. She came rushing home to find me crouched on the floor, shrieking in pain, and she immediately called 911.

A police officer was the first to arrive at the scene, and by that time I had deduced that it was most likely a kidney stone. In his attempt to sympathize with me, he said, "Oh, I hear that passing kidney stones is terrible." Thanks for that, officer. Between my bouts of pain and yells, though, I was able to go beyond my painful situation and make light of it. I jokingly offered to get the police officer something to drink, and when the ambulance came, I told them I had fallen and couldn't get up. Unfortunately they believed me when I said that and began asking me how I had fallen. I proceeded to tell them I was joking, and I explained my situation, all of this between the birth contractions of my unborn kidney stone.

Although the pain was quite unbearable at times, I never found myself wishing for things to be different. Instead, I was fully there, experiencing the waxing and waning of the stabbing agony in my back. I wasn't lost in ideas about the pain, nor was I worrying about the future. I believe deep down I knew the pain would eventually end, allowing me to relax into it, rather than resist it. In some strange sense I felt free. Even amid the discomfort, I was still able to make jokes and be myself, beyond the intolerable conditions of my body.

Reflecting back on this painful experience has shown me how much my meditation practice has blossomed. I was able to live free from the conditions I was experiencing, while simultaneously experiencing them fully. I was simply there through the passing, painful moments. Nothing extra needed to be added and there was nothing I had to do except be there.

I believe this is what our meditation practice is pointing us toward: freedom from the limited conditions of our bodies and minds.

This is not some abstract, impossible goal, but rather a real possibility for each and every one of us. Through regular sitting practice, mindfulness in daily life, and perhaps longer retreat experiences, we can all slowly liberate ourselves from the suffering of our lives, while helping others to do the same along the way.

HEALTH INSURANCE AND MINDFULNESS

In our interactions with others, gentleness, kindness, and respect are the source of harmony.

—BUDDHA

As I JUST mentioned in the previous chapter, last year I had a kidney stone. I obviously went to the hospital, and a few days later I was told to see my urologist for a follow-up. I did as I was told, and a few months later I got the best part of this whole ordeal—the bills. I do have insurance, but as usual it didn't seem to cover any of it because of some made-up preexisting condition mumbo jumbo. I had never had a kidney stone before, so how is it possible to have a preexisting condition for one? Oh, the bliss of health insurance . . .

Anyhow, I had been dealing with this for about six months and had been jumping through all kinds of hoops to get all of these bills paid. After speaking to billing and insurance representatives for many hours on the phone, everything eventually was paid, except one ultrasound from my urologist. What's funny is that they had performed two ultrasounds when I went for the visit, both for the same problem: the kidney stone. Yet for some reason they were billed separately and had two separate diagnosis codes. One of those codes matched with a preexisting condition (which, by the way, was a complaint of abdominal pain at my primary care physician from a year earlier).

Getting the bill for this ultrasound caused the flood of frustration to return. I thought I was past all this, yet there I was, back on the phone for at least two hours. To make it worse, I was talking to a representative who, of course, was giving me attitude. She was acting like she knew what she was talking about, when she clearly did not. She tried telling me I had gone to the urologist having no idea why I was having pain in my side. I had to gently remind her that I had gone to the hospital two days before seeing the urologist for a kidney stone and that it was the hospital that recommended I go for the urology visit. I have to be honest, although I'm an avid meditator I lost my patience and ended up getting snappy. Finally she got the story straight and told me she'd call me back once she figured out the problem.

It was no surprise that a week went by and I still hadn't received a call back. I picked up the phone and called her, and she again got snappy, telling me I needed to leave her a message on the machine. I guess she was busy dealing with other problems? Who knows. So I left a message, and you guessed it—they didn't call me back for the second time. I called yet again, and this time I was ready to just completely lose it and absolutely berate this unhelpful receptionist. My plan was to call her up and be really nasty. I even had the idea to threaten them, saying I was going to get a lawyer involved—anything to get them to listen to me. Of course, though, my meditative conscience chimed in, and before I made the call I was reminded that this is neither how I aspire to do things nor what I've spent years teaching people to do.

As frustrated as I was, I realized I shouldn't limit myself to these temporary feelings of dissatisfaction and discomfort, so I decided to calm myself down before I made the call. I assumed the rude receptionist would answer the call, yet this time, to my surprise, she ended up being very sweet and helpful. I calmly explained my frustrations and described all the hoops I had been jumping through to try and resolve this issue. I even apologized for having given her attitude the week before. It was a pleasant conversation, and she was very helpful. She said she was going to call me back once it was resolved, and as I'm sure you can guess, she did not—yet she *did* do what she needed to do to finally get the insurance company to pay for the second ultrasound.

The mindful, gentle approach worked.

PUTTING DOWN
THE BOULDER

*These mountains that you are carrying
you were only supposed to climb.*

—NAJWA ZEBIAN

IMAGINE IF WE were to go on a long hike, carrying a huge boulder through an unknown trail in the woods. This boulder is about a hundred pounds of extra weight and is making our hike quite unpleasant. We try hard to continue carrying it for a while, but it's awfully exhausting.

This boulder represents our sense of self—our small-mindedness with all its endless desires, aversions, judgments, and storylines—all the things we carry around with us every day. "I'm not good enough." "My life stinks." "I'm an anxious person, and I hate my anxiety." "I don't like my body." "I'm too stressed." "I'm amazing and everyone should worship me." "Life owes me something." We all walk through our lives carrying this huge burden of a self with all its problems and wants. It is a strenuous task and is quite wearing, but the good news is that whether we carry this burden around or not is completely in our control. What would it be like to put down that boulder and continue walking the trail of our lives? How much of a relief would we feel if we simply let go and put the burden down?

In this analogy, the boulder would always be there. Unlike a real boulder, which we could walk away from, this one is always with us, but we can choose to either carry it or instead observe it and say, "Wow. That's a huge freaking boulder, but I have no interest in carrying it." This is what we learn to do with meditation. We see the boulder and we keep on walking. The big rock could be anger, sadness, craving, depression, worry, or pain, or it could even be hatred or aversion toward ourselves, somebody, or something. When we rest in our awareness, we have the ability to just look at what arises: "Oh, that's interesting. Here's an angry thought," or "Ah, interesting. Anxiety is present. This is what anxiety is like." Whereas the all too common alternative is to pick it up: "I'm an angry person and I need to act or speak from this anger."

In the analogy, it's pretty simple to know whether or not we're holding the boulder. But when practicing in daily life, it's a little subtler and more difficult to discern. It can be tricky to know if we are holding on to our small-mindedness or letting it go, but with practice we are bound to learn the difference. Having an experienced teacher to help guide us and show us where we're stuck is also useful for this.

Right now, we can look and see if we are carrying something with us. If we are, let's momentarily put it down by surrendering fully to the experience of it. With that said, keep in mind that putting it down doesn't mean it's going to magically go away, but instead of becoming what we're carrying around, we can let it go and observe it objectively, as though we're walking around a big boulder instead of lugging it around. We can relate to it rather than live from it.

It's quite a refreshing experience.

MEDITATION AND STEADINESS

Ups and downs in practice are predict-
able and inevitable. The countermeasure
is always to simply persevere.

—EZRA BAYDA

As MUCH AS I love meditation, sometimes it's really hard to explain to people why I do it every day and why I dedicate so much of my time practicing it. Recently, though, I talked to a fellow practitioner in the sangha I sit with, and she explained it simply in one sentence: "Meditation brings a steadiness to my life." It may seem oversimplified, but it is a very profound and true statement.

Obviously there will be ups and downs in life, and I can say for myself that before I started practicing I would always get lost in all of them.

I would be super high, riding the wave of pleasure or happiness when things were going my way, and then I'd crash hard when things didn't go according to my master plan of how my life "should" go. My existence before practice was like an extreme rollercoaster ride. I went up and then down, up and then down. I was easily swayed by the conditions of my body, mind, and changing life situations.

Meditation, though, has given me a steadiness, allowing me to face each day, each thought, each emotion, and each body sensation with a bit of evenness and equanimity. Of course, things still happen in my life—good and bad, painful and pleasurable—but it's no longer the sickening rollercoaster ride it once used to be, just little bumps rather than huge ups and downs. I once heard author Tara Brach call it a "profound okay-ness." I love this! No matter what happens, there can be an underlying okayness that gently and compassionately holds it all. With a dedicated practice we can all be profoundly okay with our lives just the way they are, and it is such a great gift.

With the steadiness of meditation, we find we can face anything, and once we realize we can face anything, we become fearless in a certain way. What once seemed impossible to face now seems manageable because we have a center point, a still point we are coming from, rather than just being thrown around by whatever is going on. This steadiness also allows us to see that all things are impermanent. So no matter how difficult things may get, the evenness produced from our meditation practice will allow us to rest within ourselves until they pass.

We are able to rest in the steadiness within our own being. It's the consistent and unchanging awareness that just knows what's happening and can hold the very experience we're having right now.

The more we spend time here in this centered steadiness, the more we find ourselves resting there in daily life, and the less we'll be tossed around by the ups and downs we all will inevitably experience.

THE CAVE OF DEMONS

In surrendering to our deepest fears, we put ourselves in touch with the fundamental awareness of just being—the true ground that is always available to us.

—EZRA BAYDA

MANY TIMES I'VE heard the story of a Tibetan Buddhist master named Milarepa, who spent a lot of time meditating alone in caves. One day when returning from having gathered some firewood for the cool night ahead, he arrived at his cave and found it was full of demons messing with all his stuff, causing much chaos in his little home. He immediately wanted them out, yet because of his Buddhist practices he first tried being kind to them. He used compassion practices and even tried teaching them the Buddhist teachings. The demons simply laughed and continued tormenting him. Realizing this approach wasn't working, he became more frustrated, and in a fit of rage he yelled and screamed at them; he even tried chasing them out of his cave. The demons only grew bigger, laughing at Milarepa's attempts to remove them.

Milarepa finally gave up and realized these demons were not going away, so he decided instead to invite them to stay there with him. He would continue to practice as he always had, but now it would be in the presence of these menacing demons. With that courageous act of acceptance all the demons disappeared—except for one. This one was really nasty and didn't want to leave, so Milarepa went up to the demon, opened its mouth, and put his head deep inside to be swallowed up. He told the demon that if he's not going to leave he might as well just eat him and get it over with. With this wise action the last demon finally vanished.

So what's the point of this story? We all have these parts of ourselves that we don't like or would rather not have. This story shows the best way to deal with our inner "demons."

In the story, Milarepa at first tried to be nice and compassionate to the demons. He believed that if he were kind to them, they would go away. Unfortunately, his kindness was stained with an expectation—that it would make things different—and so the demons wouldn't budge. He was trying to be nice only because he didn't want them to be there. This wasn't true compassion but was instead compassion infused with both grasping and aversion. Milarepa was coming from the belief that there shouldn't be demons in his cave. That was his first problem.

It was only when he surrendered to their presence that they began to disappear. Now don't get the wrong idea; in real life our inner demons won't simply vanish by just proclaiming our acceptance of them. (Wouldn't that be nice, though? "Hey, depression. I accept you." Poof! Depression, no more!) In reality, if we let these demons arise and cease on their own, then they don't become problematic. We can accept our own demons by letting them be there. They won't just magically disappear like in the story, but they will come and go without bothering us as they once did.

Some demons, much like the last one in the story, aren't as easy to work with. Milarepa had to jump right into its mouth and allow it to eat him before this demon would vanish. For him this was an act of full acceptance and surrender. This is a very powerful approach to our own difficulties. For example, if we are having anxiety, it would be like surrendering completely to the physical experience, allowing it to do whatever it wanted (in the realm of sensations) until it finally passed. This is, of course, much easier said than done.

We will experience difficulties in our mind and body, but rather than resisting, fighting, and trying to remove them, we can try coming from a place of acceptance and see how that can transform whatever difficulty we're experiencing. We mustn't be afraid to feel uncomfortable or to lean into the things that scare us. We may find what terrifies us isn't as terrible as we make it out to be, and by learning not to struggle to remove these things, we will discover that those same problems will arise less and less.

At the very least, our inner demons can and will become more manageable and bearable than before.

THE DISAPPOINTMENT OF EXPECTATIONS

*Serenity comes when you trade expecta-
tions for acceptance.*

—ANONYMOUS

WHEN I WOKE UP this morning I was actually a little bit disappointed. There had
been big hype about a record-breaking blizzard
arriving here in New Jersey, but I woke up to find
nothing but a few snow flurries scurrying around
in the sky. It was a dusting at best. Although
I was off from my part-time day job, I still had
a yoga class to teach later that evening. There
wasn't any snow, so I couldn't cancel the class. I
was frustrated as I expected to have a whole day
of bumming around, watching movies, playing
video games, and eating lots of unhealthy food.

So when I looked out the window and saw barely any snow, I was very disappointed.

This is just one simple example of how expectations can create suffering. The reality of the situation was that it was barely snowing outside. The excitement for a huge storm, the disappointment when I woke up, and the frustration of having to go to work later on was the baggage I brought to the moment. I truly believed it was going to be different. I wanted it to be different, but it wasn't. It was what it was.

If there's any point in our daily life where we're feeling upset with a situation or a person, there's a good chance there's a big expectation hanging around. One of the most common expectations is that life will be the way we want it to be. For example, if we are heading into the city for an interview, we expect to be there on time. But perhaps on this specific afternoon, there's an accident on the bridge, and there we are, sitting in standstill traffic. In that moment our expectations are not being met, so we immediately begin reacting in a negative way. Instead of patiently waiting for the traffic to pass, we continue to tell ourselves how crappy this is and how we're going to be late to this important interview. Our mind then begins spinning into thoughts about how we aren't going to get the job, and how we'll never find a job we like, and before we know it we're completely stressed out and frustrated as we continuously believe in the worst-case scenarios our mind keeps playing in our head.

Instead, in that moment of frustration, we could ask ourselves, "What expectation am I holding on to that is preventing peace in this moment?" Usually the expectation is right there screaming at us, although sometimes we may have to dig deeper and ask a few times. The key is to be honest about the situation itself and what we're bringing to it. Once we figure out what expectation is present, such as a smooth ride into the city with an on-time arrival, we can then label and release the expectation and come fully into what the moment is asking for—for us to sit in traffic. With a peaceful mind we can then call the company we are heading over to and let them know about the accident and the traffic, staying relaxed as we slowly make our way to our destination. Regardless of which way we choose to handle the situation, we are still eventually going

236 YOUR LIFE IS MEDITATION

to get to the interview. Would we rather practice peace or continue the ancient habit of wishing life be other than what it is? It's up to us.

Having expectations is especially prevalent in relationships. Both our partner and ourselves will bring a whole suitcase full of them, which will ultimately create clashing and tension. Here are some common ones I often hear: "My partner should make me feel good all the time." "My partner should listen to me all the time." "My partner should always be supportive and be the way I want them to be." When we read these examples we may think there's no way we have such expectations, but in a moment of frustration when we're yelling and screaming, one of those expectations is most likely behind the flood of angry thoughts in our mind.

Practicing meditation encourages us to not blame our suffering on what's happening "out there," outside of ourselves in the world. Instead, it makes us point our finger at just one thing: our attachment to our own small-mindedness. We can no longer blame anyone else for our emotions or states of mind. Although others may bring them out of us, ultimately we realize they are our responsibility, and rather than pushing them away with blame, we learn to own them fully and find healthier, more peaceful ways of experiencing and processing them. It's up to us to process our own feelings. The attachment to our expectations was already present within us, as were the feelings of anger. This is the main cause of our suffering. The person or situation just forced us to experience where we're stuck. A blessing in disguise, perhaps?

If we don't take responsibility for our own expectations, and if we continue to blame the world for our misery, we will never be free. We really have to work with this and learn to honestly see our expectations and practice letting them go. Blaming others or difficult life conditions just keeps us from facing ourselves; it's a way to push our responsibility away. We can notice when we are upset and investigate our mind, and see for ourselves which expectations are present. Watch how they color our perception of reality. Study the reactions, beliefs, and physical sensations that come with attaching to these expectations, and learn how to rest at the center of it all. Through this process there will be transformation.

As I've heard before, awareness heals, and through my experience I have seen that it surely does. Try and bring a gentle, compassionate awareness to any expectations you experience today. Can you feel them fully, and allow yourself to freely observe the reactions, storylines, thoughts, and sensations that come along with them?

There's no need to judge yourself for having expectations; ironically, not having expectations is also an expectation. Just take some time to rest with them and let them be. You will eventually realize that you don't have to limit your life to your unfulfilled expectations, and you can instead try to see with clarity the reality of the situation or person.

You may find that as you let go of your expectations, you'll experience less disappointment and ultimately more peace.

THE PASSING SEASONS

There is a time for everything, and a season for every activity under the heavens.
—ECCLESIASTES 3:1

THIS PAST WINTER made it seem to me as though the long months of cold and darkness were never going to end. I remember walking to my car on many frozen days, feeling like spring was years away. But ultimately the big freeze passed, and although spring has not yet fully sprung, the warmer air surely makes it feel that way. Compared to the below-zero temperatures we experienced, forty degrees feels like summer. What a treat! The warmer air is here! We survived the brutal conditions of winter, and the snowy days are now simply memories.

In our lives there are going to be times, situations, emotions, and states of mind that seem unending and unbearable. Whether it's anxiety or depression, grief for a lost loved one, chronic pain, or even a horrible job situation, it will all change. We must always keep this in mind, especially when we are going through it, because if we start indulging in thoughts such as, "I can't stand this," "I can't take this," "It shouldn't be this way," or "I shouldn't have to deal with this," we are only going to drive ourselves crazy and add much unnecessary suffering. Instead, we can simply experience the difficulty. The difficulty itself is already enough, and although it may seem unbearable and might in fact be quite unpleasant, we can absolutely face it and get through it. We may even be able to find some peace, compassion, and wisdom along the way.

Our meditation practice teaches us to directly experience the rawness of our lives. The good news is that we have to face only one moment at a time, and if this moment is unpleasant, we can face it openly and relaxed because we know it's going to change—it has to. Even in the practice of meditation we sometimes may get sore knees or an unbearable itch. It seems horrible, and we immediately want to get some relief. We believe if we don't move our leg, or scratch that itch, we are going to die! But the truth is that we *won't* die, and as uncomfortable as it may be, we can still learn to relax and just be fully there with it. In fact, the best thing we can do when we are facing discomfort or difficulty is to stay as fully present as we can, bearing witness to the pain we are experiencing, making sure our minds are not making things worse.

For those of us currently going through something that seems unbearable, we may want to try relaxing into the discomfort. We don't need to wish that it be any other way, and we can try letting go of all attempts to fix what's going on. We can make friends with the physical discomfort and let go of all the thoughts about it that are making us suffer even more. At the very least, we can try labeling the thoughts passing through our mind, allowing for some space. Rest in the moment fully and see what happens.

The internal winter will pass and spring will bloom.

So, for now, just be patient and kind.

VISITING LAKE POCASSET

No man ever steps in the same river twice,
for it's not the same river and he's not the
same man.

—HERACLITUS

EVERY YEAR I go away with my family to our vacation home in Wayne, Maine. For those of you who don't know (and I'm assuming that's all of you), Wayne is about twenty minutes from Maine's capital, Augusta. My family has been blessed with a small cabin right on a small lake called Pocasset. The cabin is owned and shared by my father and his siblings, and each family is designated two weeks each summer when they can go and enjoy the bliss of Maine.

Every August when I get out of the car after that long six-and-a-half-hour to eight-hour drive (depending on traffic), I go down on the dock and gaze out at the lake. To me, it seems exactly as it was the year prior. It's almost as though it's never changed since I was a little boy. Of course, this is obviously not the case. The truth is that the lake has always been changing and flowing, and "Pocasset" is just a term of convenience—a name given to the inexpressible reality that we call the lake. Water has constantly streamed from one lake, through our lake, and off to another since the lake was birthed. This means every time we've gone to Lake Pocasset, there has been completely new water flowing through. Even on any given day, it's a new lake anytime I jump into the water. It's never the same exact lake. Sometimes the wind is blowing north, sometimes south, yet the water is always flowing, so it can't possibly ever be the same.

In our lives, we have labels for convenience so that we can function and let people know where we're going. But again, the convenience can never capture the essence of what it's pointing to. If I investigate deeply enough, there is actually no Lake Pocasset, even though I can clearly see it every year when I go there. Does this make sense?

Let me give another example. Suppose we look up at the stars on a clear night. It's very easy to spot the Big Dipper. We've been taught that the group of stars that literally looks like a big dipper is in fact *the* Big Dipper. When we gaze up into the stars, we immediately recognize it as such. Even if we tried not to see it, there would be no way of missing it. To us, the Big Dipper is real, and the few stars we see grouped together in the sky comprise it, yet it is just another convenience—a label pointing to a reality. The fact is that there is no Big Dipper—there never was. There's simply a group of stars emitting their glow from light-years away.

During my college years, I remember reading a great article by philosopher Hilary Lawson called "Stephen Hawking Is Wrong." Lawson claimed scientists such as Hawking put "closures" on reality as they divide the world into things, explanations, and theories. We mistake these closures for reality itself, losing reality in the process. Lawson explained that:

> . . . the world is not a thing or a combination of things, for these categories—these

closures, as I call them—are the outcome of our descriptions. Instead, the world is open and it is we who close it. Through our closures we grasp the openness of the world as things, and out of these things we build stories and models through which we are able to intervene. But these stories and models are not the world, nor could they in principle come close to being the world.

In the same way scientists place closures on what is naturally open, we, too, place a ton of closures on ourselves, believing in our thoughts and judgments of ourselves, rather than experiencing the reality of who we *really* are. A large part of practicing mindfulness has to do with learning to see these closures and practicing letting them go. For example, we have our names, and they are conveniences allowing us to function in this world. Yet, similar to the lake, our sense of self has never once been the same. Our bodies are completely different with every passing year. Our beliefs have evolved and changed, and so have our habits and reactions. Even on any given day, there are so many thoughts flowing through our mind, and so many emotions surging through our body. We are never static.

There is only the movement of life, constantly flowing through each of us—as each of us. This point is extremely important to understand because if we can understand that we're not as solid as we think, then we'll realize we are never stuck. No matter what we experience, internally or externally, that experience *has* to change. When this realization runs deep into our bones, we no longer cling to happiness, comfort, youth, and health, because we know very well those things will change. At the same time, we won't be as afraid of discomfort, sickness, and things we dislike, because they too will ultimately change. Understanding life from this deeper level allows us the possibility for true peace, joy, and gratitude, as we are no longer fighting life or trying to manipulate it to our liking. Instead, we are welcoming it as it comes, just as it is.

We can finally relax into the lives we're actually living, all the while doing our best to engage in it wholeheartedly.

We must see our identities for what they truly are: a convenience no different from Lake Pocasset or the Big Dipper. This doesn't mean we need to remove this convenience, but rather learn to use it when necessary, always keeping in mind that we're so much more. Alan Watts said it best when he explained, "You are a function of what the whole universe is doing in the same way that a wave is a function of what the whole ocean is doing." So yes, we are partially a convenience, but we are always simultaneously much larger.

It's important to remember this point, learn to trust in that, and let go into your bigger self.

WE'RE GETTING
CLOSER TO
THE END

One of my favorite subjects of contemplation is this question: Since death is certain, but the time of death is uncertain, what is the most important thing?

—PEMA CHÖDRÖN

ALL TOO OFTEN I see and hear people who are always rushing through their days. If it's early in the morning, they can't wait until the end of the day. If it's wintertime, they can't wait for summer. If they begin schooling, they can't wait until it's over. As soon as they start work, they can't wait until they are back home. It seems as if we are programmed as human beings to be more interested in being somewhere else, rather than being where we are.

Unfortunately, though, our lives are swiftly passing us by, and as I often say to my meditation students, "The only place you are rushing to is the end of your life." We must realize our death is inevitable, and our time of death is unknown to us. It's even possible that today may be the very last day of our lives. We may not make it to the end of the day, to next summer, or to wherever it is we are constantly rushing off to in our minds.

We must learn to appreciate our lives, moment by moment, and equally take in the good and bad. A tough or boring day at work, an argument with a family member, or sitting in a traffic jam are all things we'd rather speed through and forget, yet if we knew it was our last day, how special would it be to sit in traffic or spend a day working at a crappy job? It may not seem to be special now (or while you're experiencing it, for that matter), but when faced with your own mortality, intense gratitude, joy, and appreciation can definitely emerge.

Instead of rushing through the day today, take the time to literally wake up and smell the roses. Go ahead—smell them!

Allow yourself to indulge in all the five senses throughout the entire day, seeing all the sights, hearing all the sounds, and feeling what it feels like to be fully in your body.

Welcome all experiences, pleasant or not, as if today were your last day ever of experiencing life.

Appreciate everyone and everything.

This life is so very special.

It's about time you wake up to your rare and beautiful existence.

USING MINDFULNESS TO LEAN INTO DISCOMFORT

When we stop "taking the edge off" and those sharp edges come back into our lives, we begin to witness how leaning into the discomfort of vulnerability teaches us how to live with joy, gratitude, and grace.

—Brené Brown

MINDFULNESS is an excellent tool for leaning into the discomforts of life, ultimately helping us liberate ourselves from the ever-changing conditions of our body and mind. Remember, mindfulness is our ability to be aware of the present moment, without the filter of judgments, storylines, or labels. It is an open, receptive, direct experience of whatever's happening—right now. The tool used for mindfulness is our own ability to be awake, awareness itself, which is like a mirror reflecting whatever is put in front of it. Much like a mirror, our awareness simply knows what's happening, even before our thinking mind comes in with its ideas, beliefs, and judgments. With mindfulness we learn to rest in "things as they are," connecting with a peace and joy beyond the conditions of our body and mind.

Unlike popular belief, the purpose of using mindfulness in daily life is not as a self-help tool that helps us fix ourselves or become a better person, and it's definitely not a method to get rid of parts of ourselves that we don't like. Although these may be real results of a steady mindfulness practice, they are not the reasons why we do it.

The true meaning of practicing mindfulness is to learn how to relax into and make friends with the present moment, regardless of the conditions present. This clear seeing from a receptive, unbiased awareness helps us realize that with mindfulness we can hold any experience, pleasant or not, with equanimity and compassion. In doing so, we'll connect with a peace and

joy beyond good and bad, right and wrong, pleasure and pain, and so forth. We'll also learn to
see that all things are fleeting, and with practice
we'll become, as poet T. S. Eliot once said, "the still
point of the turning world." From this still point
we'll have a stability and clarity that will allow
us the freedom to choose how we act or speak, in
any situation of our life, regardless of what our
emotions and thoughts are telling us. This is true
freedom, and the good news is that it's right here
waiting for us in the present moment.

Let's face it: given the nature of our existence,
our lives are bound to be uncomfortable. Not only
do we age and get sick from time to time, but ultimately we will be separated from everything and
everyone we love and cherish. On top of this, we
often have to encounter difficult emotions, as
well as people or situations we dislike—a bout
of anxiety, an annoying coworker, a toothache,
or a traffic jam, just to name a few. When faced
with discomfort, though, the last thing we ever
want to do is simply experience it. Normally our
minds immediately fill up with fearful thoughts,
judgments, ideas of how to fix the discomfort,
or even cravings for a quick fix, such as intoxicants or distractions. This intense urge to avoid

discomfort, combined with our inability to fully rest in it, leaves us feeling even more uncomfortable and actually makes what already felt bad feel even worse.

Without mindfulness, any discomfort we face has the potential to bring about a whole lot of unnecessary suffering. So what steps can we take to lean into discomfort when it arises? Try this simple exercise: The first step when facing any form of discomfort is to come fully into the present moment. We see what our body actually feels like without adding any judgments or storylines. Where is the discomfort? Where do we feel it in our body? These questions will point us directly to the different sensations we're typically not aware of. Next, we notice what our mind is saying. What thoughts are we believing that are making this initial discomfort even worse? Some common thoughts we may find are: "Life shouldn't be this way." "I can't take this anymore." "Nobody should have to feel like this." "I hate when this happens."

By believing in these thoughts we actually make the situation feel much worse. These thoughts are common, and if we notice them in our mind, we can simply label them for what they are. For example, if we are feeling anxious and our mind is telling you how much we hate feeling this way, then just label that thought by saying, "Having a thought that I hate feeling this way." This easy labeling exercise creates a space between what's true and what our thoughts are saying about that truth, and allows us to come into the actual feeling of discomfort. We continue labeling our thoughts over and over again in order to try and stay with the physical sensations of what we are actually feeling, rather than our storylines about it. From here, we can relax our body, deepen our breathing, and simply let whatever arises be there. With immense friendliness and warmth, and a lot of loving attention, we hold the discomfort in our body as we would hold a crying baby. We get to know the actual feeling and learn to be with it in an intimate and welcoming way.

We can also add a dimension of compassion to this exercise by wishing that all beings who are experiencing the same discomfort we are be free from it. Once we finish sending out a wish of loving-kindness we are ready to simply get back to whatever it is we have to do next in our day, whether it's work, washing dishes, taking care of our kids, or going for a walk. We just show up fully to where we are, allowing the discomfort to join us.

It's important to understand that this exercise of being present, labeling thoughts, and wishing others freedom from the discomfort we experience is not a way to get rid of the discomfort or fix it, but rather a way for us to learn how to relax into it—to be at ease with it. Once we learn how to relax into the discomforts of life, we will no longer spend so much time trying to escape from them, which finally allows for a truly peaceful mind.

MOVING FROM SUBJECTIVE TO OBJECTIVE

In what is seen, there should be just the
seen; in what is heard, there should be
just the heard; in what is sensed, there
should be just the sensed; in what is
thought, there should be just the thought.
—Buddha

WITH MEDITATION we learn to rest in our awareness. We rest in our ability to know that, right now, the present moment is like this. Within our awareness are the objects found in awareness. Thoughts, emotions, sensations, smells, tastes, and sights are all objects of our awareness. On a normal day we are very much identified and tied up with these objects. We cling to them and believe they're who we actually are.

Practice is about coming back to awareness itself and shifting our identities from the objects in our awareness to the awareness itself. Awareness is much like space. No matter how much we try to hit space, nothing happens. Whatever happens within space, space is unaffected and can hold it all. Similarly, our awareness can hold every experience of our lives, while still remaining unmoved.

All we have to do is simply practice becoming aware, and the good news is that we don't have to try to be aware; we were born aware and awake. It's natural and simple. Once we let go of distractions, awareness is there. Even when we're fighting to let go or are struggling with what's present, it's still there watching, silently observing it all. I invite you to try for one minute to *not* be aware. Try whatever you think will make you lose this ability.

Ready?

Go!

Were you able to not be aware? Not likely! Awareness is here to stay, and although our awareness may get distracted or hijacked, it never actually goes away.

To clarify further, our meditation practice allows us to make a shift from a subjective to an objective experience. Normally we identify with our body and mind; it's who we believe we are. Everything is seen through this subjective filter of "me" and "mine." We become the owner of it all—*my* thoughts, *my* feelings, *my* body, *my* pain, *my* pleasure, and so on. But in our practice we make the shift from this subjective reality to a more objective one. In other words, we experience thoughts as just events of the mind, and emotions as shifting bodily energies. We do the same with the sensations of the body, and even with the entire body itself. We let go of all this self-grasping—of calling everything me and mine—and we simply experience this moment as it is, without any sense of ownership. If there are thoughts, we notice the thoughts. If there's anger, we simply note the angry sensations. If there's happiness, we just notice it. If we are sitting in meditation and our knees hurt, we take note of the uncomfortable sensation.

At first this will be a challenge, as we are so used to identifying experiences as our own. If there are bad thoughts, we feel as though we are bad. If we're obsessing over something we can't change, we feel bad about it. When we make the shift to an objective experience of life, thoughts become thoughts; anger is only an uncomfortable sensation, as is pain. It's as if there's a big burden being lifted. Everything is still the same. We still feel all of it—the pain, the emotions, and confusion—but the burden of it being who we are is no longer there.

We must become like a scientist who experiences reality as objectively as possible. The only difference is that what's going under the microscope, so to speak, is you.

Enjoy the research!

THE VIRUSES
OF THE MIND

Emotions are contagious. We've all known it experientially You know after you have a really fun coffee with a friend, you feel good. When you have a rude clerk in a store, you walk away feeling bad.

—DANIEL GOLEMAN

CAUGHT A flu-like virus a couple of weeks ago. For about ten days my chest was tight, my head was throbbing, and I felt beyond exhausted. I was laid up in my bed like a dead slug, barely leaving my room. Just making the walk to the bathroom required immense willpower; the fatigue was extreme.

As with all viruses, there was really nothing I could do except wait it out. Sure, I could take some medication to ease the symptoms, but that could only do so much. My only choice was to rest and surrender to the unpleasant symptoms until the virus finally passed. With time and much patience the symptoms slowly became more bearable, and my fever finally cooled down. About two weeks after the start of the virus, my energy was coming back, and I was finally feeling back to normal. What a relief!

Our body isn't the only place that can get viruses—our mind can too. Try thinking of difficult emotions and thoughts as viruses of the mind. Slowly they infiltrate our being, causing all kinds of unpleasant physical symptoms such as tightness in the belly, chest, or throat; restricted breathing; and dizziness. Other symptoms can include obsessive thinking, the desire to speak harmful words, and even cravings to act unwholesomely or compulsively.

There are all kinds of viruses of the mind. Some examples are anger, aversion, greed, hatred, jealousy, anxiety, and even intense cravings. Most of the time they enter quietly when we're off guard and not being mindful. Sometimes we catch one from a coworker, or a rude stranger, and other times our own thinking creates its own. Regardless of what causes them, the discomfort from the symptoms can be brutal and oftentimes destructive.

Much like actually being sick, the best thing to do when we notice one of these viruses in our mind is to be very awake and surrender fully to its symptoms. Instead of believing what it is trying to tell us, and acting or speaking from it, we can instead realize its presence and relax into its symptoms. We can examine what the virus in our mind is having us believe or what it wants us to do, and learn to see those things as simply symptoms of the virus, rather than as who we are.

Sometimes there may be remedies, such as deep breathing or other meditation techniques.

Yet much like real viruses, the best antidote is to bring an open, receptive attention to them, allowing them to run their course until they pass.

We can try to relax and rest with the discomfort until we are feeling better—otherwise we may spread the virus to others!

BEGINNER'S MIND

In the beginner's mind there are many possibilities; in the expert's mind there are few.

—SHUNRYU ROSHI

WHEN WE HEAR the word "beginner," most of us immediately believe we are lacking something and are worse off than the so-called "experts." I, personally, have noticed a negative stigma placed on being a beginner, and I often see this firsthand in some of the yoga classes I teach. I've had many new clients say they want to start yoga but believe they need a "beginner's" class. Although there is nothing wrong with starting at a beginner's level, and this is exactly where they *should* be, it's almost as if some seem ashamed or disappointed in themselves, especially when

268 ■ YOUR LIFE IS MEDITATION

they're around those who have been practicing for a while.

Although we may think it's never good to be a beginner, and we'd much rather be an expert, with the practice of meditation it's better to have the mind of a beginner. Here's why . . . .

Suzuki Roshi once said, "If your mind is empty, it is always ready for anything, it is open to everything. In the beginner's mind there are many possibilities, but in the expert's mind there are few." If meditation is new to us, we have the advantage of what Suzuki Roshi called the beginner's mind. Because we have no clue what meditation is about or what it can do for our life, we have no preconceived notions or conceptions and are fully open to the instruction of practice. With no ideas or expectations, we have a more curious and receptive mind, which is essentially what any serious meditation practitioner is looking to cultivate.

Experts, on the other hand, are full of knowledge, which is not necessarily an issue, but this fullness tends to be limiting and has the potential to create a narrow view of the practice. There's an old Zen story that shows this point well:

A famous Zen scholar went to ask a Zen master about the practice of Zen. Upon his arrival, the scholar kept going on and on about everything he knew and had learned, endlessly spilling out his opinions and beliefs on the subject. While the scholar kept on yapping, the Zen master began pouring tea for his visitor. He poured and poured and continued pouring until the water finally began overflowing from the scholar's cup. Realizing this, the scholar told the master to stop pouring, as the cup was full. The Zen master wisely explained to the scholar how he was much like the cup—full of ideas—and if he wanted to learn anything from him he needed to "empty his cup." How could the master teach the scholar if the scholar was already full of his own preconceived notions of what practice was about? This was a great learning experience for the scholar.

Ultimately, this empty beginner's mind is the state of mind we want to have for the rest of our lives, because as soon as we feel like we know how things *should* be, we are already caught in our ideas and beliefs.

The expert mind that *knows* is not only limited to meditation but actually carries over into our daily lives. We think we "know" our signifi-cant others, our family members, our friends, and the way life is supposed to be, but in reality the only thing we are certain about is our beliefs about them. What we think we know is simply our mind's definition—a filtered view of reality. With our so-called expert mind, we feel we know how others are going to speak, how they will act, or how they are going to react. Because of this, we are never able to see the world as fresh and new in each moment, for it is blocked by our thoughts. It's very limiting and causes a lot of unnecessary suffering.

Even if we have been meditating for a while, we can still try to see each sitting as completely new. Although we may think otherwise, we really don't know what this meditation will bring. Maybe we will feel bored, or maybe we will burst out in tears for no reason. It's possible that our body and mind may slip away and we can expe-rience the deepest part of our being. The truth is that we just don't know. Every time we sit we have the opportunity to throw away what we think we know. Toss it all out the window! Each moment brings us something new. Each moment is a once-in-a-lifetime experience that will never happen again. No matter how many times we sit with ourselves, we will always be beginners. Our mind will be different, as will our body. With a curious mind, we can let go of everything and experience the moment as it truly is.

What's our body like right now?

Let's look and see.

What's our mind like right now?

Oh, how interesting!

If we notice pain, then we simply experience it just as it is. We don't need to make a fuss about it, or add a storyline about what we think it is. The expert mind will want to explain what the pain is, how you got it, and what we can do about it, whereas the beginner's mind simply experiences the painful sensation. Will it change? Will it go away?

Who knows?

It's best to look and find out firsthand what will happen.

FACING THE WALLS OF IGNORANCE

The doorstep to the temple of wisdom is knowledge of our own ignorance.

—BENJAMIN FRANKLIN

W E ALL HAVE a desire deep down to be free from our suffering. We all want to have peace and joy in our lives. Unfortunately, though, it seems actually *having* them is a rare case. Being peaceful and loving all the time is no doubt an inspiring ideal, but the reality of our lives never seems to come close. The truth is that a large part of our practice is simply learning to see very clearly what's preventing us from the true peace and joy we seek. By seeing the thoughts, beliefs, and expectations that block us from the peace and joy that is readily available to us, we are gaining wisdom into the walls created by our own ignorance.

When we feel full of anxiety or disconnected from life, we can ask ourselves: "What exactly is it that's not allowing me to feel peace in this moment?" "What expectation is here that's not allowing me to experience the joy in my life?" Although it may seem like observing our reactions, thoughts, and whatever else may be blocking our hearts from opening is doing nothing, with awareness we have an opportunity to heal these blockages and melt away the walls of ignorance. Of course, this doesn't typically happen right away, but if we continue to bring an open, receptive, nonjudgmental awareness to that which blocks us from the peace and joy in our lives, something will eventually soften, and transformation will transpire.

When we don't give our habitual patterns ground to stand on, they cannot endure and they fall apart. It may be the hundredth time we open to the same difficulty, or it could be the millionth time. Whenever it happens, it happens. Remember, transformation happens in its own time and is not up to us, so rather than getting stuck over and over again, habitually lost in our confusion and neuroses, we can instead let go and simply watch, without judgment, what our mind is doing. We can observe the storylines and experience the emotional baggage without becoming engulfed in it.

With careful observation and daily mindfulness we will begin to see that what actually prevents us from true peace and joy is our small-mindedness that wants life to be the way that it wants it to be. Truth, with a capital T, is life in this moment, just the way it is. Ignorance, on the other hand, is our ego's interpretations and filters that keep telling us life shouldn't be the way it is.

We must face these walls of ignorance and bring them down in order to experience Truth. It's essential to see clearly and continuously let go of what prevents us from the reality of our lives and from the reality of true peace and joy. Sounds and thoughts coming and going, body sensations arising and ceasing, the movement of the breath in and out—it's all just the flowing river of life. We may not always like where life is flowing, but we always have the choice to let go into it.

We can embrace situations, people, and emotions we don't like, as we face the walls of ignorance we've created and slowly allow them to melt away.

MEDITATION IS
NOT SELFISH

*Meditation is not a selfish thing. Even
though you're diving in and experiencing
the Self, you're not closing yourself off
from the world. You're strengthening
yourself, so that you can be more effective
when you go back into the world.*

— DAVID LYNCH

THE PROCESS OF doing work on ourselves
through meditation, mindfulness, and longer retreats leads some people to believe meditation is selfish. Our significant other, friends,
or family may see us making sure we have time
to sit in meditation every day, or they may see
us making sure we have a free weekend twice a
year for a retreat, and they may believe we are
simply being self-centered—only worrying about

ourselves. If the true essence of practice is misunderstood, then of course meditation can be very self-oriented, as it becomes solely focused on our personal inner peace and liberation, but this is *not* the way of a true meditation practitioner.

In Zen Buddhism, however, meditation is practiced not to save ourselves, but rather to save all beings. In fact, at the end of every sitting, a Buddhist typically chants four vows, the first one being: "Sentient beings are numberless; I vow to free them all." Of course we're practicing in order to liberate ourselves—if we can't free ourselves from suffering in our own life, how can we help anyone else?—but ultimately our goal is to use what we learn in our practice to be more available to reduce the suffering in the world around us.

It's true: sitting in meditation oftentimes makes us feel peaceful and gives us an inner stability to face life, and if we were to only sit in meditation every day, carrying the benefits of a clear, relaxed, and compassionate mind with us throughout our day, this actually would be enough for our practice to be selfless. How is this possible? Think of it this way: Think of the last time an angry person walked into a room at work.

Regardless of whether that person spoke to us or not, we would absolutely sense his frustration and aggression. This misery is quick to spread and can have devastating results. That one miserable person could put a few more people in a bad mood. Those people then bring it home with them and are quick to snap at their family members, causing the family to be frustrated and upset. The newly frustrated children then go to school unhappy and spread that unhappiness some more to their friends, peers, teachers, and so on. This cycle could continue on and on and on.

Now, imagine the Dalai Lama were to walk in to the same place the angry person was in. It wouldn't be hard to feel the stillness and peace radiating from him. This peace and joy would spread to people's homes, families, schools, and so forth.

In order to understand how meditation is not selfish, we must understand that everything we do—every thought we have, every action we act on, every word we speak—has an effect on everybody; everything creates a ripple that shoots out into the entire universe. That's how interrelated we really are. On top of this, if we are always

focused on ourselves, we will never even realize
there are other people who are suffering. There
will be no room for anyone else when our hearts
and minds are full of self-centeredness.

If we can keep all beings in mind as we practice, then meditation isn't selfish at all. Also,
understanding our interconnectedness to all
things deeply helps us realize that as we sit in
meditation, everybody sits in meditation. That
may seem absurd, but when studied deeply it
makes perfect sense. As we attain liberation, all
beings are liberated, because the more at peace
we are with ourselves, the more peace we share.
Through our practice we affect every form of life
we encounter. That's why it's always good to finish any meditation or spiritual practice by recit-
ing the wish for all beings to be free from their
suffering. Or even finish by imagining ourselves
sharing the positive energy we created in our
practice to help alleviate those who are suffering.
Anything to help be reminded that meditation
isn't just about us.

If we use meditation as just another means to
get comfortable, feel pleasure, or obtain security
in our lives, then it indeed becomes selfish. That's

just the ego in control again, but if we are able to use it in a way to rest in the present moment without getting lost in our neuroses, and then help other people do the same, then I believe we are on the right path.

WATCH OUT FOR THE TIGERS!

Joy comes from appreciation. Appreciation comes from paying attention. Paying attention is the practice of Zen.

—Anonymous

THERE'S AN OLD Buddhist story about a man being chased by tigers—when he finds himself at the edge of a cliff. As the tigers get closer he leaps off, hoping to escape the savage beasts. While midair, he looks down only to find more tigers waiting below. Luckily there happens to be a wild vine growing on the side of the cliff. Thinking fast he grabs hold of the vine and grips it tightly for dear life. He's now stuck with no means of escaping. Looking up he sees tigers; looking down he sees the same. To make matters worse, he notices a little mouse gnawing on the end of the vine. It's only a matter of time before the mouse chews right through it and causes the poor man to plummet to his death. Looking around in despair, the man happens to see a small strawberry bush, with some fresh ripe strawberries, growing right next to the vine. The man plucks a strawberry and takes a bite. How sweet and delicious!

This story is, of course, about our own lives. Every moment since birth we have been hanging from the cliff, always moving one step closer to the end. None of us make it out alive. In the story, the man knew his time was almost up, yet he was still able to find joy and be fully present for his experience of a delicious strawberry. He wasn't lost in thoughts about the tigers above and below him, nor was he obsessing over the mouse gnawing at his only means for survival. Instead of hanging in fear and waiting to die, he chose to fully live.

When we look at our own lives, are we able to say we are fully living? How many of us are afraid to do so? Are we courageous enough to stand up in the face of uncertainty, death, chaos, and suffering, and feel joy rather than curl up in fear? Many people don't know how to feel joy, while others don't think they deserve to feel it at all. Most of us are too distracted by the tigers to even realize there is a tasty strawberry right there next to us, waiting to be plucked and enjoyed.

Recently, I went for an outdoor run with my son. As we were running up and down the streets of my neighborhood, we noticed a tiny Laughing Buddha statue in a small garden. It seemed as though the garden had not been tended to in a long time and the poor cement Buddha was completely covered in mud—but it still had a huge joyful smile on its face. I paused with this tiny joyful statue covered in mud and thought, what a wonderful message. To me, this mud-covered Buddha statue represented our potential to live our lives joyfully, even being fully covered in the mud of our difficulties, sorrows, and pain.

I am reminded of a talk I heard where the Zen teacher encouraged students to show up to their cushions covered in mud. We should come to the zendo and sit, even when we feel ashamed or discontent with our practice—like the traditional image of the lotus flower being at home in muddy water. We too can blossom where we are planted.

We practice meditation to bring ourselves into this moment and to find that tasty strawberry, regardless of the tigers surrounding us. Taking a bite of that strawberry is a continuous choice we make to either appreciate our lives in the moment and to feel that joy, or instead grasp tightly to the vine, fearful for our lives. Enjoying the strawberry doesn't mean we feel good all the time, but it *does* mean we have deep, genuine appreciation for this very life we are living, regardless of the flavor. We must learn to find the strawberry in the chaos of our daily lives. It's sitting right there in front of us—always. All we have to do is simply pluck it and take a bite.

How delicious!

ONE BODY*

People normally cut reality into compartments, and so are unable to see the interdependence of all phenomena. To see one in all and all in one is to break through the great barrier which narrows one's perception of reality.

—THICH NHAT HANH

THERE'S A CONCEPT in Buddhism that's called *anatta*, which translates to no-self. This is one of the most important teachings in Buddhism and is often misunderstood. When most people hear the teachings on no-self, they immediately grow confused. Here I am, sitting right here. How can there be no-self? On a recent retreat, one of my Dharma brothers gave a talk on this

---

*This chapter is dedicated to the life and practice of James Kozan Furey, whose Dharma talk inspired this chapter.

subject. Instead of using the term *no-self*, though, he exchanged it for interconnectedness. Using interconnectedness, rather than no-self, made the teachings more accessible and less abstract, at least for me.

I truly believe any real spiritual path is trying to get us to see our interconnected nature. Typically we deal with life from this little island we call *self*. From this one point of view this sense of self seems separate from everything and everybody. It needs to take care of and protect itself, putting its needs before anyone else's. It wants what it wants. It wants life to just be the way that it wants it to be. This is a major cause of our suffering, yet we don't know there is an alternative.

As our practice deepens, we start realizing and experiencing this interconnected nature more and more. The truth of the matter is that we're not really as separate as we may think. Although we can clearly see we are different from each other, this doesn't mean we aren't interconnected. Let's take our body, for instance. Each one of our bodies has fingers, knees, a nose, a mouth, eyes, a brain, a heart, etc., all of which are completely different. Each part is distinct and has unique jobs to assist in the life of our bodies. It's true: on one level there is separation and difference, but upon further investigation we also find that the sum of these parts works together in harmony as one body. Just as our one body has many parts that are not truly separate from each other, so too is each of our lives part of the one body of the entire universe.

Another way to look at this is to think of waves in the ocean. Each wave is unique, separate from the other waves around it, yet on the deepest level they are all part of one big ocean. One wave is separate from the other yet fully the same.

There is a great practice to help remind us of our interconnected nature. This works especially well when around difficult people. Anytime we experience a difficult person, we can try repeating "one body" to ourselves in order to remind us that we are equal parts of the same whole. This helps us view this difficult person in a new light and allows us to move away from our small-minded, self-centered view, to a larger, spacious possibility. Of course, this person may still very well be a major pain in the ass, but that's simply their *suchness* in that moment. When we see this person as ourselves, though, from the larger perspective of one body, we will find that we want to relieve this person's suffering, rather than shrug them off in anger. Remember, if someone is miserable to be around, they must be feeling even more miserable and unhappy with themselves. Think about it. If we're happy, what would be our motivation to bother other people? There wouldn't be any.

The teachings of no-self—understanding the interconnectedness of the one body—help us remember that any difficult person is no different from ourselves, and although one body may sound like an abstract theory, the truth is that we experience it all the time. For example, if we think of a time when we surprised somebody with a gift and we felt happy, this is an experience of one body. We aren't feeling our happiness; we're actually feeling the happiness they're feeling. In that moment there is one body and no separation between ourselves giving the gift and the person receiving it.

Interconnectedness is not some far-off goal we need to attain. It's right here, but we have to work with this sense of I, with all its problems and judgments getting in our way. With practice it is possible to experience an amazing depth of interconnectedness. We must continue to practice, opening ourselves more and more each day to the truth of *anatta*.

We can try and remember this teaching throughout the week, and when we find ourselves in a difficult situation with somebody, we can silently repeat "one body," reminding ourselves of our interconnected nature. This may not rid us of all our troubles, but it may help us gain a new perspective on the person we are dealing with. Having this larger perspective, we may find ourselves spontaneously saying or doing something that can bring peace to this difficult person's heart, transforming our relationship with them.

As always, test it out and see what happens.

SIMPLIFY, SLOW DOWN, AND SEE CLEARLY

In an age of speed, I began to think, nothing could be more invigorating than going slow. In an age of distraction, nothing can feel more luxurious than paying attention.

—PICO IYER

MEDITATION HAS BEEN around for thousands of years as a way for seekers of all faiths to become intimately familiar with the deepest aspects of their being. It is an ancient art used to cultivate concentration, wisdom, and compassion. Although the task of meditation is extremely simple, most find it quite difficult. This is because the true purpose of meditation is not immediately apparent. Meditation is not a way to escape from life, nor is it a "quick fix" that will make our problems magically go away. It won't give us mystical powers, and it's not going to permanently stop our wild monkey mind. Rather, meditation is a way to simplify, slow down, and see clearly.

We simplify our lives by taking the time every day, whether five, ten, or twenty minutes, to stop our normal daily routine of running errands and making appointments, and simply sit still, watch the movement of the breath, and rest in the present moment. When thoughts arise they are accepted and released, rather than judged, suppressed, or acted upon. (It's important to understand that thoughts are *not* a problem in meditation.) Simplifying ourselves in this way allows us to be free from distractions, putting us face to face with the present moment, whatever it may be. By continually doing this over and over again, the mind learns how to rest in the direct experience of the present moment, instead of continuously becoming lost in self-centered thoughts and judgments about it—"I like this," "I don't like this," and so on. Resting in clear, open awareness, we are able to watch our experience like one watches clouds pass through the vast open sky.

As we simplify our lives, we also learn how to slow down. During meditation we gradually, over a long period of time, begin to slow down our thinking mind. This does not mean our mind is forever inactive or comes to a complete halt, but rather that we will tend to dwell less and less in the content of our mind, and instead rest in the reality of our moment-to-moment experience. Of course, there may be moments of stillness, where the mind is not moving at all, but this is not the main point of our meditation practice. It's important to understand that we *don't* have to stop the mind; we need only to change our relationship to it. By slowing down, we are actually able to see our thinking mind clearly when it arises, either choosing to follow it or not. This simple ability allows us to become the master of our actions and speech, rather than having our mind master us into acting or speaking. This is true freedom.

When one simplifies and slows down, the result is seeing clearly—mindfulness of the present moment. Only by seeing clearly can wisdom arise in one's life. What is it that we are seeing clearly? We begin to see attachments and aversions, thoughts and feelings, and habitual behaviors and reactions. We get to know our loving-kindness and compassion, along with our neuroses and suffering. We become familiar with *all* aspects of ourselves, recognizing when our mind creates suffering, and learning (with a dedicated, patient practice) how to gently and compassionately let it go, or at the very least find ways not to escalate it.

As our practice with the Three S's (simplify, slow down, and see clearly) deepens, we find more space in our mind to breathe, even amid intense moments of suffering. By simplifying ourselves, we learn to slow down and see each moment clearly.

Only when we see clearly are we able to free ourselves from the shackles of our judgments and storylines, allowing us to experience each moment of our lives in an open, honest, and relaxed way.

PROFOUND PEACE AT THE GROCERY STORE?

Zen is not some kind of excitement, but concentration on our usual everyday routine.

—SHUNRYU SUZUKI

ALL OF US want to live a peaceful life, and we will do all kinds of crazy things to try and get it. Usually, though, our efforts seem futile. Maybe we get temporary peace of mind, but then something changes and we come right back into the messiness of life.

In order to experience true peace, it's important to understand what peace actually is. If we think peace is a nice, warm, fuzzy feeling that we get, we'll be highly disappointed repeatedly, because feelings, even peaceful ones, are impermanent and cannot last. It's true: meditation will leave us feeling very calm and serene at times. We might even find that we leave our meditation cushion feeling completely blissed out, ready to love everyone and be fully receptive to whatever life hands us—but when we get back to reality and our significant other, for instance, doesn't share the same spiritual high or gives us attitude about the mess we left in the kitchen, immediately bliss runs out the door and leaves us standing there alone, flustered, and defensively arguing back. Peace is nowhere to be found.

This is not the true peace we are shooting for in practice. The real peace comes from not wanting life to be any different than it is in this moment—having no craving, as the Buddha would say. We'll start to dwell in true peace that's not just a feeling when we're able to let go of the attachments to these cravings for life to be other than what it is. It's a peace beyond feelings and beyond the conditions of our lives.

I vividly remember having rested fully in this peace one day when I was at the grocery store food shopping. Usually I can't stand going to the grocery store because no matter how many times

I go, I just can't seem to find what I'm looking for. And what's sad about that is that I get the same thing every time I go. But on this particular afternoon, there I was with my cart, walking through the store. There weren't any thoughts about where I was going to find groceries or how I didn't want to be there by myself. There were no cravings to be anywhere else but exactly where I was. There was no desire for life to be other than what it was. I was fully present in the most ordinary way, yet it was one of the most profound moments of peace I've ever experienced. I was just present—nothing special, blissful, or out of this world . . . just simply being.

The good news is that we all have this ability to experience this profound simplicity anytime, even when there are intense cravings in our mind for life to be other than what it is. We can still let that go and just be with what is and experience that. We must stop searching for some magical, blissful peace, experience, or feeling we can grasp onto, because we're just going to be continuously disappointed. Instead, we can let go into the moment—*every* moment—being there fully for our lives and acting naturally in accordance with the conditions present right now.

Remember, peace is ordinary and is nothing special, and it's always present if we just let go of the judging mind with all its cravings.

THE LIMITATIONS
OF PERSONALITY

Watch your thoughts, they become your words; watch your words, they become your actions; watch your actions, they become your habits; watch your habits, they become your character; watch your character, it becomes your destiny.

—ANONYMOUS

ALL OF US identify with our personalities. It's our sense of self and what makes us unique. There's nothing wrong with identifying ourselves as our personality, as this is how we function together in the world. But our personality, like all things, is a product of causes and conditions.

Even our normal day-to-day moods are based on the conditions of that specific moment. If we find ourselves stuck in traffic and have to be at an important meeting, the personality will become enraged and will make our body tense. The personality will always limit what's actually happening by spitting out beliefs and judgments. To make things worse, the personality will even make judgments about the personality itself, causing even more confusion and suffering.

When we believe only in our personality, we will have a very limited view of reality. When things go our way, we're in a good mood, but when things don't go our way, our mood is lousy and upset. We end up going up and down on an endless rollercoaster ride with the conditions of our lives.

Meditation allows us to practice going beyond our limited sense of self, connecting us with our true nature. With our awareness we can actually watch the personality arising and ceasing based on certain conditions. Some teachers call this continuous arising of a personality as "selfing." When we are around someone who is unpleasant, we can watch the personality come in and immediately filter the reality with negative judgments and storylines. We can then investigate how limiting these views are. The difficult person is frozen as a "bad person," and there are no other options for them. Even if they come in and are happy, the limited views instantly overlook that and think something must be up. "Why are they being so nice today?" "They must be up to something." In this way, moment by moment, the personality not only filters the present moment reality but also limits it to only our views, desires, fears, and worries.

It's important to reemphasize that these limitations of the personality are not problems. This is how everyone's mind functions. The practice is not to get rid of it, or feel sorry for having a limited personality, but to see it clearly and not let it limit our lives any longer.

Let me tell you about a recent example of my working with my own limited personality. A few weeks ago I woke up to go to work, only to find it had snowed almost a foot. No one else was awake, and I knew if I waited I still wouldn't be helped, as we only had one shovel anyway. It was up to me to shovel the steps, walkway, sidewalk, and drive-way, as well as clean the snow off all four cars. My personality immediately began spitting out bitter thoughts about how I was the only one who ever cleaned up the snow, and about how stupid it was that there was only one shovel. On and on my personality went. "Everyone else is cozy in bed, and here I am shoveling heavy snow," I grumbled.

I observed my mind as it kept complaining about the cold, and all the hard, uncomfortable work that came with the wintery job. But beyond my personality with all its complaints, the reality of the moment was that there was snow on the driveway and the cars, and it needed to be shoveled. That's what the moment was asking for. Because of my dedicated practice to mindfulness, I was able to acknowledge my whining personality and let it continue spitting out its negative comments, and instead of indulging in the thoughts and letting them limit the reality of that moment, I picked up the shovel and began shoveling the snowy mess. Oh, the bliss of true freedom!

Our personality will always be limited, but there is something beyond it: the timeless awareness which holds life as it truly is in the present moment. We must train ourselves to see clearly and rest in this awareness when our personality arises and limits our perception of the moment. With patience and discipline we can allow it to fall away. I believe this is what the teachers mean when they say "die on the cushion." In other words, to continuously allow who we think we are to be born and then observe that version of our "self" passing away. When we don't give our thoughts, moods, and feelings (which we normally identify with) any ground to stand on, they have no choice but to fall apart. A deep mindfulness practice makes this process more clear, and we eventually understand this not only on a conceptual level, but also more important at an experiential level.

Instead of limiting our lives to our personality we can choose to be fully in the moment, and act appropriately according to our clear awareness of the situation itself.

It's not easy, but we can simply try our best.

THE BATTLE OF THE TWO WOLVES

We are what we repeatedly do.
—WILL DURANT

THERE'S A WONDERFUL Native American story I've heard many times of an elder in a tribe, talking to his grandson. He explains to him how inside each one of us there is a constant battle going on between two wolves. There's the bad wolf, which is greed, hatred, ignorance, anger, lust, craving, jealousy, etc., and the good wolf, which is joy, peace, kindness, generosity, compassion, and so on. Hearing about these two wolves, the grandson asks the elder which one wins. He answers by telling him, "Whichever one you feed the most."

Every day, with every action, word, and thought we indulge in, we are feeding one of those two wolves. If we're honest with ourselves and can really pay attention, even just for one day, we'll see which wolf we are feeding. Whether we are aware of it or not, we are practicing something every moment. It's important to understand that we are what we practice the most and, more important, that we get better at what we practice. If we look deeply at our lives and pay attention throughout the day, we can see what we are practicing most often. Are we practicing selfishness and self-hatred? Worry? Anger? Or kindness, compassion, and receptive awareness?

If we are looking for true peace in our lives, it's important to feed the right wolf. This doesn't mean we don't get angry or experience any of the bad wolf's emotions or neuroses, but it's really the relationship to those negative experiences that will do the feeding. If we become angry and are full of anger, speaking and acting from the anger is feeding the wrong wolf. Whereas if we experience the anger and know that anger is present, and instead speak from a place of wisdom, compassion, and kindness, then we are feeding the right wolf.

Our practice is more than just our cushion—more than simply sitting in meditation. This can't be overemphasized enough. It must extend into how we live our lives. I'm not saying we have to be perfect, but we must continue doing our best to practice feeding the good wolf. Continue cultivating the qualities of compassion and kindness, extending them not only to ourselves but to everyone we encounter.

Which wolf have we been feeding? Today, let's take an honest look.

TRANSFORMING AVERSION

If you change the way you look at things,
the things you look at change.

—WAYNE DYER

O N ZEN BUDDHIST retreats there is a job known as the *jikido*, or the timekeeper. The *jikido* is responsible for maintaining the order of the retreat by keeping a keen eye on the time. He or she must wake the practitioners every morning, ring bells and clap boards at appropriate times, and signal the beginning and ending of meditation sessions with gentle gongs on the singing bowl or taps on the bell.

The jikido always needs to know which scheduled activity is coming up next and identify the correct Zen instrument needed to signal that activity. Three gongs here, two claps there, and after some sittings they even have to lead the group in chanting.

This past spring I signed up for a weekend retreat. I saved up money, found coverage for work, and was ready to relax and dive right into a weekend of meditation and mindfulness.

The jikido was definitely not a thought that had crossed my mind. I had been on retreats before, and where I usually practice, being the timekeeper had never been an option. Typically, the monks, nuns, or volunteers would keep time while the retreat participants practiced intensely.

On this retreat, however, I was appointed jikido. In an instant, my mood changed from excited to devastated. *I paid good money to come here, and I have to keep the time?* I thought to myself. *How am I supposed to go deep into meditation if I have to keep looking at the clock?* Of course, I ignored these thoughts in front of my teacher, put on a gentle smile, joined palms, bowed, and agreed to take on the position.

Although on the outside I seemed to be volunteering, my mind was far from it. The whole first night my thoughts raced around in circles, complaining and justifying my frustration. I could only observe the opinions and self-righteousness coming and going in my awareness. What else could I do as I sat there watching the clock tick by one second at a time?

Saturday morning was even worse; I had to get up at 4:45 a.m. to be sure that I could wake everyone up by 5:00 a.m. So much for getting rest. That morning, though, I decided I was going to let go of my resistance and be as present as possible for my newly assigned job. Watching the time, hitting the bells . . . I was going to use all of it to keep a relaxed attention of the present moment. The point of meditation is to be completely awake and aware in the present moment, anyway. Isn't that what I was being asked to do as the jikido? In fact, I had to pay even closer attention.

I went through the rest of the day with complete presence and focus on the tasks at hand. When ringing the bell, I felt the mallet in my hand and fully listened to the vibrant sound of its voice. I found ways to go deep into meditation by trusting my internal clock to keep time. By the afternoon sitting period, I found myself eager to ring the preparatory bells. The whole process was becoming a meditation in and of itself, which brought me great peace and joy.

Is this not the purpose of our practice? Transforming the very life we are living? The job was the same all weekend. It never once changed. What changed was my relationship to it. Once I let go of my aversion and all the "shoulds" and "should-nots" of what it meant to be on retreat, I found great joy in the very thing I couldn't stand.

One could easily say meditation changes everything, yet paradoxically doesn't change anything at all. Much like the job of the jikido, the difficulties we encounter throughout our lives will always be the way they are—nothing more and nothing less. We can spend our whole lives struggling with them, or we can change them by changing ourselves—by changing our relationship to them.

When we drop the way we think things ought to be, we may be surprised to find peace and joy in the very things we once couldn't bear to face.

COMING HOME
TO YOURSELF

Wherever I'm going, I'm already home.
—JASON MRAZ, *LIVING IN THE MOMENT*

ULTIMATELY, our entire meditation practice is about coming home to ourselves and being at ease with what we find.

This ease is not only limited to the fun, happy parts of ourselves, but also includes our most horrifying and darkest parts. With the practice of meditation we are not trying to renovate or fix our home, nor is it about buying a new home and selling the old one. It's about learning to come to our true home, to the truth of ourselves just the way we are.

But what is our true home? Our true home is beyond our thoughts and emotions; it's much deeper than that. We come home to the loving awareness and sanity that lies beneath. This is our true self—our deeper self. It's the part of ourselves that's still there when states of mind come and go, and when difficulties arise and cease. It's been there all along. When things seem to be falling apart in our lives, we are being directed toward our true home: the indestructible part of ourselves. So falling apart isn't necessarily a bad thing; it's only the unstable parts that are falling away.

To come home to ourselves is to be fully in the moment with whatever's present. We're not coming home to feel good, as we don't always feel good. We come home to just be there, to be at ease with whatever's present, pleasant or not.

As we sit in meditation, we cultivate an openness and receptiveness to whatever arises. The more we sit with ourselves, the more at ease we'll be, regardless of what conditions are present. This is what coming home to ourselves is about, and the good news is we can always practice it, whether we're happy, glad, sad, mad, or in pain.

THE BROKEN JUKEBOX IN YOUR MIND

Insanity is doing the same thing over and over again, but expecting different results.

—ATTRIBUTED TO ALBERT EINSTEIN

A S OUR MEDITATION practice deepens and we begin to bring the mindfulness of meditation into our daily life, we'll start to see what's going on in our body and mind more clearly. Although we will notice thousands of thoughts running through our mind every day, we'll find there are only a few common themes among them. Imagine our mind as an old broken jukebox that, for some reason, only plays the same few records day in and day out. These "records" are the deep-seated beliefs we have about the world and ourselves. Some familiar tunes may be: "I'm not good enough," "I'm unlovable," "Life is unfair," "Things shouldn't be this way," and "I am broken and need to be fixed." In reality, these deep-seated thoughts don't have any real truth to them, but we take them to be the ultimate reality, and then we live from that false perception.

Generally, these records are created in child-hood. Maybe some of us didn't receive enough attention from one or both of our parents, so now we are constantly seeking out approval, as the record of "I am worthless" continues running the show. Many, if not all of our thoughts, actions, and words will be based on this deep-seated belief of unworthiness or lack. Still, some beliefs may come from traumatic life experiences, such as getting diagnosed with a terminal illness, getting abused, being stalked, or experiencing a near-death accident. These examples have the poten-tial to create new records such as: "Life is out of control," or "I am not safe," which impacts every aspect of our lives by narrowing our reality to a very small, cramped place.

Much of meditation in daily life is observ-ing and learning the main records being played in our mind. What are the common themes of our thoughts and daydreams? Are we building ourselves up or putting ourselves down? What do we believe that isn't the actual reality of this moment? We must look and see for ourselves.

Keep in mind, whatever we find isn't wrong. We're not a bad person for having these records; it's just the present condition of our mind. We're not looking inward to judge or berate ourselves for having this deep-seated conditioning, but instead we're realizing exactly what is driving our thoughts, actions, and words, and ultimately learning to free ourselves from them.

What makes this difficult, though, is the amount of emotional baggage that comes along with these records. The last thing we want to do is dive headfirst into the overwhelming feelings that created the tunes to begin with, but part of the meditation path is to turn toward that which we've turned away from for so long, and I will tell you from experience it's not always pleasant. But with practice, patience, compassion, and humor, we can experience these difficulties and go through them, releasing ourselves from their grips.

Sure, the tunes may still play from time to time, but their seduction and strength will lessen, and we will gradually live a life free from the old habits and patterns our mind once created.

THE POOL OF FREEDOM

A little progress each day adds up to big results.

—MOHSIN JAMEEL

THERE IS A large pool of freedom. This pool is empty and needs to be filled completely. We fill it up by continuously letting go of our small-mindedness, letting go of our limited beliefs and judgments.

While sitting in meditation we watch a thought come up, and as soon as we realize we're thinking, we can just say, "Ah, yes. Thinking." When we let it go, we can simply come back to the present moment to the direct experience of ourselves sitting. Eventually, we can bring this same type of awareness with us throughout the day and let go of unnecessary or harmful thoughts all the time—especially when the mind is limiting our perception of reality.

Every time we let go of thoughts it's like taking a little eyedropper and pouring a few drops into the pool. Drop by drop you continue to fill this large pool of freedom.

No effort is ever wasted; any little drop will add more water to the pool. Maybe we're standing in front of the fridge at night and we want to eat something "bad," like a cupcake or a cookie, to cover over some dissatisfaction or unease.

If we are able to notice the craving and let it go, that's one drop.

And then, maybe the next day, we let go of a thought about someone we dislike. We notice "Ah, yes. Thinking how I don't like this person. Thank you for your opinion, mind"—and let go of the thought, adding yet another drop into our pool of freedom.

It's going to take a long time to fill the pool— perhaps an entire lifetime—but just continue putting those drops in, day by day.

Don't worry about when the pool will finally be full.

Just keep putting water in, drop by drop, every day.

THE WAVING CROSSING GUARD

*Spread love everywhere you go. Let no one
ever come to you without leaving happier.*
—MOTHER TERESA

THE CENTRAL THEME of this book is, of course,
that meditation practice is not limited to our
cushion but is rather fully expressed in daily life.

I am reminded of this continually by a man
who was a janitor at my local high school. He's
now retired and working as a crossing guard on
the corner of a street I used to live off of. Because
I am in that area often, I tend to drive by him a
lot throughout the year. The first time I saw him
he was waving at everyone like a maniac. He was
flapping his arms, yelling, "Yeah!" or "Have a nice
one, buddy." At first I didn't know what to think,
and to be quite honest I actually thought it was a

324 ■ YOUR LIFE IS MEDITATION

little strange. But after I saw him several times, it ended up being kind of fun.

I actually began to enjoy driving down that street because I knew he would be there pointing his finger at everyone, waving, and telling them to have a good day. This waving crossing guard found a way to make his job special, and he impacted everybody because of it. Every morning and afternoon anyone who drives by is bound to see him and all the other people honking, waving, and smiling back at him. A retired janitor became a crossing guard and now brings immense joy to what he does. Although he probably doesn't meditate, he sure knows how to live the practice in his daily life.

Clearly it doesn't matter what we are doing with our lives; instead, it's *how* we're doing it that counts. There was an analogy from the movie *Enlighten Up!* in which one guru explained how anyone could bake a cake, but the attention and love we have when baking it can vary greatly, completely changing our inner experience during the process. We could bake a cake for a stranger or a lover, or as an offering for the Divine. Of course, at the end of the day, it's still just baking a cake, but the inner world is completely different depending on why we're doing it and whom we're doing it for.

In the same way, it's what we bring to our job, not necessarily what we're doing, that's going to express our practice in daily life. We may very well have the most boring, mundane job in the world, but how can we make it special? How can we bring peace and spread joy to those around us?

This week, or even just today, explore this and put some of your ideas into practice.

Living your practice is always a possibility.

IF IT ARISES,
IT BELONGS

*I am human, and I think nothing human
is alien to me.*

—TERENCE

*No amount of meditation, yoga, diet, and
reflection will make all our problems go
away, but we can transform our difficulties into our practice until little by little
they guide us on our way.*

—JACK KORNFIELD

I ONCE HEARD A story about a man who came to
see the Buddha hoping he could help him get
rid of the problems in his life. He went on and
on about everything going wrong in his life. The
Buddha patiently listened and after the man was

finished the he replied, "I'm sorry but I can't help you with any of those problems."

The man became upset and questioned the Buddha, "You are the Buddha, the enlightened one. How can you not help me get rid of any of my problems?"

The Buddha answered, "Everyone in the world has 83 problems. One problem gets solved and another comes along. I cannot help you with that. What I can help you with though, is the 84th problem."

The man asked, "What is the 84th problem?"

The Buddha wisely answered, "That you want to get rid of your 83 problems."

Meditation master Ajahn Sumedho teaches: "If it arises, it belongs." This quote is something to be contemplated and lived each moment of our lives, and it can help guide our meditation practice. I feel it is also the main point of the story and epigraph above. If anything arises, inside or outside of us, it should be embraced with awareness, bowed to with respect, and seen for what it is. We can use each moment of our life to learn about the wide array of experiences we have within this human realm. Absolutely everything that happens belongs here and is part of the ride.

The point is there isn't anything that shouldn't be in our lives, even if it is absolutely painful, difficult, or terrifying. What's in our lives is just simply what's in our lives. It's a fact. So rather than waste time struggling to remove what we don't like and grasping what we do like, we can instead embrace the changing flow of our lives and let go of the obsessive need to control, resist, and struggle with it. We can use our meditation practice not as a way to get rid of our difficulties, but rather as a way to let go into the direct experience of each moment, pleasant or not.

From this clear, direct seeing with our awareness, we can allow our deepest wisdom to take over, rather than go through our lives lost in our limited, conditioned mind.

The most common stumbling block I see people struggle with when beginning a meditation practice is the desire to gain or attain something—the what's-in-it-for-me attitude. This comes from the belief that what's already present isn't enough, or is lacking in some way.

Life is full of troubles and many of us are still holding on to the idea that it's not supposed to be this way. This is a major cause of our suffering and dissatisfaction!

I can't tell you how often I am asked, "How will my life change if I meditate every day?" My answer is generally (with an obnoxious smile), "It won't." Of course, on one level, I'm joking. There are an abundance of benefits that come from a disciplined practice. There's no denying this! But the truth is we aren't trying to change anything. In fact, it's the attachment to this self that fights how things are that blocks us from the very peace and equanimity we are searching for. Paradoxically, it's only through letting go of this yearning for all of life's problems to go away, that we finally discover the natural, open awareness we were born with—a peaceful, awakened state beyond the conditions of our lives. If we are too busy running away from the fact that life is difficult sometimes and needs to be some other way, then we will never be still long enough to actually see this.

Tibetan Buddhist teacher Chögyam Trungpa Rinpoche put it this way, "Go through it. Experience it. Give in to it. Then the most powerful energies become absolutely workable rather than taking you over, because there is nothing to take over if you are not putting up any resistance." Clearly, the effort in our practice is most effective when it's used toward embracing our lives, rather than struggling against them.

So remember: if it arises, it belongs.

A SINGER'S
LAST GIG

*Live every day as if it were your last
because someday you're going to be right.*
—MUHAMMAD ALI

M Y FATHER-IN-LAW'S band has been around
for quite some time. They were very popular in their younger years and are still filling up
venues today. It's always an enjoyable night when
I go to see them play.

I recently found out that the singer has
stage 4 lung cancer, and because of the location
of his tumor, it's inoperable. Knowing this news,
I decided to go see them play last week. With
the doctors giving him one to two years max,
along with chemotherapy and radiation treat-
ments on the way, I assumed this would be their
last gig together. While I was at the gig, I began

334 of YOUR LIFE IS MEDITATION

watching him intently, wondering to myself how it would feel to be in his shoes. He's been playing music with this band for the majority of his life, and that night could quite possibly be his last show ever.

Imagine that.

Doing something we love for our whole lives, and knowing it could be the last time we're ever going to do it? It's very intense. I tried to wonder how much presence and gratitude he had that night. How special it must have been. Although he was clearly in much pain, the preciousness of that concert must have been unspeakable.

This experience made me think about how I was living my own life. This man had at least been told how long he has, so he has a good idea of when to expect his own passing. But for most us, we have no idea when our lives will end. For all we know it could be tomorrow—hopefully not, but life is always uncertain.

Watching him sing that night made me wonder if it's possible to live each and every moment as if we knew it were our last day alive. Can we experience the preciousness of each moment? Can we live fully and deeply with full appreciation and gratitude? Can we stop planning and rushing around and simply be there for the most ordinary moments of our lives? I believe so.

As you sit in meditation today, try fully experiencing whatever is happening. Be with it intimately, and truly cherish it. This moment will never happen again. For all you know, this could be your last day on this beautiful planet.

Feel the specialness of this once-in-a-lifetime chance to experience life in a human body, and gently hold that thought throughout the day with each step and each breath. Feel the warmth of the sun, hear the birds singing, smell a flower, and, most important, don't forget to laugh with friends and family.

TWO METAPHORS

Metaphors have a way of holding the most truth in the least space.
—ORSON SCOTT CARD

I AM NOT A huge fan of traveling into New York City, but when I do, I almost always take the bus to Port Authority. For those who don't live around NYC, Port Authority is, I believe, the nation's largest and busiest bus terminal. Buses from all over the Tri-State area come in and out of this terminal, bringing passengers and commuters both in and out of the Big Apple.

When we sit in meditation, it's like sitting at the center of Port Authority. Each thought is a bus getting ready to pick us up and take us away to its next destination. If we get on the bus, it will take us for a ride until it gets us to where it's headed, and then it will drop us off. Sometimes the destination is not a preferred stop. Other times, it's a one-way trip to a brick wall.

In meditation, we allow the "thought-buses" to pull up all throughout the session, but instead of hopping on one of them, we simply let them pull up and drive off. Many buses will visit us, but we do not have to get on any of them.

Sometimes we may find ourselves sitting in the backseat of a bus, and we won't even remember having gotten on it. No big deal. When we find ourselves on one these thought-buses, immediately tell the bus driver to pull over, then simply exit and come back to the Port Authority—the present moment.

Here's a second image: Let's imagine ourselves as a little seed of an apple tree. We start off being thrown into a deep hole and are buried with dirt. It's dark and cold in this hole, and every so often we get flooded with water. Over time we start breaking out of our seedling shell and begin pushing our way up through the dirt. In time, we reach the surface and poke through the ground— and finally we are able to see the light of day. From here it will take perhaps four to eight years to finally grow into a full-sized tree. Once we make it that far, we may eventually start bearing fruit, and after all these years of hard work and dedication to grow and provide these tiny apples, we realize we must freely give them all away. Try to imagine putting that much time and effort into something only to freely give it away; years of work only for all the fruits of our efforts to be handed out to others.

The life of an apple tree is a wonderful teacher for how to live a meditative life. Live to give. All the kindness, wisdom, compassion, and gentleness cultivated in meditation are to be freely given away to all who come in contact with us throughout our lives. This is much easier said than done, yet this is our practice. We must learn to be generous and give away all we receive from our meditation practice. And the paradoxical secret is this: when we give everything away, we have nothing left but immense joy.

BIRTH CONTRACTIONS

Emotion only lasts in our bodies for about 90 seconds. After that, the physical reaction dissipates, unless our cognitive brain kicks in and starts connecting our anger with past events.

—JILL BOLTE TAYLOR

I TYPICALLY GET A Slurpee once a year on 7-Eleven's national Free Slurpee Day: July 11—literally 7/11. But four years ago, instead of coming home with an ice-cold watermelon Sour Patch Kids Slurpee, I was in the hospital welcoming my baby boy into the world. He was born at 8:19 a.m. on the morning of national Free Slurpee Day, two weeks before his expected due date. He was and still continues to be the sweetest treat I could ever ask for, infinitely more satisfying than a lifetime of Slurpees. (FYI, a week after his birth I did finally go get my Slurpee.)

Prior to Mason's birth my wife and I had signed up for a four-week class that introduced us to what we could expect before, during, and after birth. To be honest, I hadn't been nervous about the whole process until I took the class. We were given Birthing 101, from start to finish, with graphic images and videos to get the full experience. What a sight.

Although a plethora of topics were covered, the most prominent one in my mind was the lecture on contractions. As I'm sure we all remember from sixth-grade health class, the female body experiences intense contractions in order to push a baby out. As painful as they may be, the good news is that they don't last very long. A typical contraction will last about a minute, going through a building phase until it hits its peak. It then gradually begins lowering until the pain eventually disappears completely. I am in no way denying how excruciating the pain may be, but its intensity is fleeting and workable, which is why hospitals offer Lamaze classes, which give women breathing techniques to make it through the severe bouts of pain. These techniques allow a birthing mother to focus her mind on the breath rather than the discomfort of the contractions.

With the birthing process in mind, we can imagine all our frustrations, desires, and any other uncomfortable emotions or situations we experience as simply painful yet impermanent birthing contractions. Just as a contraction builds up, hits its peak, and ultimately goes away, so too will all our difficult experiences arise and fall away. If it's possible for a person to get through the whole birthing process, one contraction at a time—regardless of how painful it may be—then it's absolutely possible for each to get through any painful mental arising that life may throw our way. Of course, the anguish or distress may not last only a minute, but perhaps a few days, months, or even years—but even so, all experiences will eventually hit a peak and then begin to change.

The next time you experience suffering of any kind, do your best to let go of the thoughts about it and simply experience the sensations it brings up in your body. What does it feel like to experience this difficulty?

Remember how, similar to bearing birthing contractions, it's possible to stay with the uncomfortable physical sensations until they peak and eventually fade away. You don't need to try and escape or get rid of the painful feelings; instead you can experience them fully until they change.

Much like giving birth, focusing on our breath is quite useful, but whatever helps you sit through it is fine. I can't promise your efforts will birth a child, but sitting through your difficulties will surely have its own gifts to celebrate.

MINDFULNESS AND RENUNCIATION

*The inner work is in letting go, in the
renunciation of the wandering mind, of
afflictive emotions, of the idea of self.*

—JOSEPH GOLDSTEIN

AGAIN: THE PATH of meditation is not limited to just sitting and following the breath.
Hopefully, this far along in the book, it's starting
to sink in! Our true meditation practice is right
smack in the middle of our daily life, doing whatever it is we are doing. If we are walking, we just
walk. If we are eating, we just eat. If we are sitting
in traffic, we just sit in traffic. The only difference
between a typical person and someone practicing in daily life is the attention and precision in
which things are done. Attention and precision

come directly from two important tools: mindfulness and renunciation.

Remember, mindfulness is our ability to pay attention to the present moment, without judgments or labels. With mindfulness our awareness is like a mirror, simply reflecting whatever is placed in front of it. Mindfulness doesn't get involved with concepts such as right and wrong or good and bad, but rather sees everything clearly, just the way it is. From this open state of mind there is clear seeing, which allows us to relax into the moment and respond appropriately to the present circumstances.

Although concentration is needed for mindfulness, mindfulness is not concentration. Concentration is typically a goal-oriented practice, keeping the mind focused on one object to attain a special state of mind. Mindfulness, however, has no goal, as it is a full presence of mind. Instead of narrowing our awareness to one object of meditation, the entire present moment becomes our focus. If our mindfulness practice is based on a goal attained at some future time, we are literally missing the whole point of the practice. Don't worry about results, attainments, or goals; simply be open to and aware of the present moment. This is mindfulness.

Renunciation, on the other hand, is our ability to let go of resistance to whatever we find ourselves facing each and every moment. We literally renounce, let go of, struggling with our lives and ourselves, learning to open our hearts even when everything is screaming within us to close it down. Renunciation teaches us to stay, keeping us from our normal means of escaping life when it becomes uncomfortable or painful. It retrains us to be with the uneasy feelings underlying all our painful habits, addictions, and harmful behaviors, rather than quickly finding expedient means to get rid of them. The more we practice renouncing resistance and escape, the more we learn not to take the bait of our habitual ways—the bait that keeps us from fully experiencing the present moment, no matter what its flavor may be.

Renunciation, like many of the meditative practices, is much easier said than done. It sounds like an inspiring and profound idea to not act out when you are angry, or not grab a glass of wine when you feel the onset of anxiety, but the actual practice is not so easy. This is because we have been habituated to escape discomfort at all costs, and true renunciation is rarely comfortable. Liberation is not just rainbows and unicorns.

As Ajahn Chah explains, "There are two kinds of suffering: the suffering that leads to more suffering and the suffering that leads to the end of suffering. If you are not willing to face the second kind of suffering, you will surely continue to experience the first." In this case, the first type of suffering is acting out on our impulse to escape. Our quick fixes become addicting and ultimately lead to an endless cycle of suffering. On the other hand, facing the discomfort without acting out, although uncomfortable, leads to freedom and peace.

Together, mindfulness and renunciation lead to a peaceful life. Mindfulness allows us to actually be in the moment, and renunciation gives us a chance to fully rest there without struggle or resistance, regardless of the circumstances we may find ourselves in. Although difficult at times, I encourage us all to practice wholeheartedly.

The world will appreciate your practice, no matter how small.

PRACTICE
BEING KIND

My religion is very simple. My religion is kindness.

—THE DALAI LAMA

GIVEN THE STATE of the world we are living in, kindness is desperately needed. But it is wishful thinking to imagine the world will magically transform without taking some level of responsibility. As Gandhi once said, we must be the change we want to see in the world. This means our practice must begin with ourselves. If we ourselves cannot be kind to and accepting of every part of ourselves, we cannot expect it out in the world. How we treat the darkest parts of ourselves is how we will treat it when it's met outside of us. For example, if we look away from our own pain, we will most likely shy away from painful situations in the world, but as we learn to hold our own suffering, we become more able to hold the suffering of others. What we do for ourselves, we do for the rest of the world. This is why the practice of meditation must include being a little bit kinder to ourselves.

Normally in our daily lives, when things happen to us or when certain thoughts or sensations arise, we immediately judge them. We are quick to add harsh judgments and storylines to the problems we face, and we're always adding more suffering to our initial pain. In fact, most of us have really nasty judgments toward ourselves, such as: "I'm not good enough," "I'm unlovable," "I'm fundamentally flawed," "I need to fix myself," etc. There can be no peace in our lives if this gentleness or kindness toward ourselves is missing. How can we be at ease when we always feel something's wrong?

In meditation we practice being kind by allowing whatever arises to be there. This is the ultimate form of friendliness toward ourselves. Whether it's anxiety, pain, sadness, desire, craving, or an endless stream of wandering thoughts and fantasies, we don't judge ourselves for anything we experience. The more we practice this unconditional openness to our own experience, the more our brains become hardwired for kindness. This means more and more kindness will begin leaking into our daily life, making us less judgmental and naturally kinder to others.

During these difficult times of division, aversion, intolerance, and cruelty, it is of dire importance that we cultivate and maintain this kindness as best we can, practicing being kind every single day through meditation, while allowing ourselves to simply be who we are, without any harsh judgments or wishes to be different. Each day we can practice extending this kindness to others, meeting them exactly where they are, and allowing all people and situations we encounter to be who or what they are without limiting them to our own ideas or beliefs.

Remember, just like us, other people want to be happy and don't want to suffer. And also just like us they may mistake suffering for true happiness, and do harmful things in the name of this so-called happiness. In fact, we can never know what someone is experiencing, so it's best to be kind even when others may not be. Sometimes an act of kindness can melt away another's suffering. At the very least, it won't escalate it. Throughout my years of practice, I've known many miserable people who I'm sure appreciate my not causing them extra stress by reacting to their stress.

It is possible for us to dedicate the rest of our lives to spreading kindness, both to ourselves and others. For today, set an intention to practice responding kindly to everything you encounter. Meet yourself just as you are, and greet others joyfully with kindness, even if they are not returning it back.

THE POWER OF LABELING THOUGHTS

Don't hate the arising of thoughts or stop the thoughts that do arise. Simply realize that our original mind, right from the start, is beyond thought, so that no matter what, you never get involved with thoughts. Illuminate original mind, and no other understanding is necessary.

—BANKEI

ONE OF THE first things we're taught in meditation is how to acknowledge and label our thoughts. There are two basic ways of doing so. One is just lumping them all together in one thing called "thinking." Anytime we have a thought that distracts us from our breath or object of meditation, we simply say, "Ah, thinking," and bring our mind back to the object of focus. Another method I've also learned is labeling the thought by its specific content. For example, when we realize we're having a thought about what we have to do for work tomorrow, just say, "Having a thought that I need to get this done at work tomorrow." Or if we're having an anxious thought such as, "Oh my god, what is this test result from the doctor going to be?" we can simply label it by saying, "Having a thought about the test result," or "Having an anxious thought." With this method there is no "right" way we have to do it. The important thing is that we're learning to see our thoughts as simply thoughts. Both of these methods for labeling thoughts are very powerful practices. They are not only simple to do, but they can be done anytime.

As we label our thoughts, we no longer identify with every thought that comes to mind. Thoughts don't become who we are, but instead are simply experiences passing through our mind. When we label thoughts, we start to see the difference between thoughts and awareness itself—and we allow ourselves to have more space around them. When we're able to label our thoughts in this way, we then have a choice to either listen to them or let them go. It's especially useful for any addictions or habitual patterns of behavior or thinking.

For all of us, there are people in our lives to whom we react habitually. For instance, every time we're around them, we immediately give them an attitude. We quickly feel threatened and shut down no matter what they may say to us. If we're able to see these thoughts very clearly and be honest with ourselves at this time, we may find the deep-seated beliefs hidden behind the knee-jerk reactions. Like, "I never truly feel heard." We may also be able to see our expectations and belief systems, such as "You need to listen to me on demand." If left unobserved, we will forever be trapped in this limited view of them, but if we are able to see these patterns, we can start to label them, creating space for new ways of being.

Remember, if we continually do the same thing (like use our mind angrily, for instance) over and over again, we're going to get the same result. If we want a better relationship with this person yet continue to react in the same way, we're just going to stay stuck. By labeling and letting go of these thoughts, we're thrown face-first into the physical reality of what's actually happening; we get to experience the reality of the moment. We are then able to see what's happening beyond our thoughts and emotions. This allows for a new way of being.

We practice labeling thoughts in seated meditation, and then we start bringing it into our daily lives. It's possible for us to be constantly aware of what's going on in our body and mind. If we find certain thoughts are harmful, we can practice labeling them, and try to relax into the reality of that moment. It's not always easy to do, especially with thoughts we are very attached to, but remember, we're always free to choose to indulge or release a thought. Once we are able to see the thoughts driving our behavior, then we are able to work with labeling them and ultimately letting them go.

Don't underestimate the power of labeling thoughts; it is a transformational practice.

For the rest of today, try watching what you do and how you react, and see which thoughts are governing your speech and behavior.

Try letting go of any thoughts that are limiting or harmful, and then see what happens when you let them simply be by labeling them.

Don't judge the thoughts or indulge in them. Instead, experience their impermanent nature, and rest fully in the freshness of the moment.

THINGS ARE SELDOM AS THEY SEEM

First appearance deceives many.

—PHAEDRUS

O N MY LAST ten-day retreat, I remember being very envious of one of the other practitioners. She is always at the retreat center and has been on every retreat I've ever done. I'm always wondering how she goes on so many retreats and how she's always there, as I'm almost sure she has a family. Regardless, she's a committed practitioner, and on this retreat I vividly remember looking over at her only to find her sitting peacefully like a Buddha during every meditation period. Even between sittings, when we usually do walking meditation to give our legs a break, she would continue sitting there, perfectly still, looking relaxed and radiating peace.

I, on the other hand, suffered greatly.

After only twenty minutes I'd be stretching my legs, pissed off that they hurt and that I was still unable to deal with the body pains of sitting, even as an experienced retreat practitioner. My envious eyes kept gazing over at this woman, who seemed to be sitting still like a mountain. From my perspective, her retreat was going well, while mine seemed to be a disaster. Throughout the rest of the retreat I kept getting mad whenever I looked at her, jealous of her peacefulness and ability to be still.

At the end of the retreat, when we were all finally able to talk after the excruciating ten days of silence, we sat around in a big circle and were free to share about our retreat experience. When this particular woman joined her palms, signaling her turn to share, I recall saying to myself, "Oh great, let's hear how amazing her retreat was." To my surprise, she suffered greatly during the entire retreat, sharing with everybody traumatic details from her past. Although she believed she had dealt with the painful memories and gut-wrenching emotions, to her surprise, all of it had come surging back with a vengeance. Her entire retreat was plagued with difficult memories and intense emotional upheavals.

I was stunned.

Hearing her share her experience was a complete shock to my assumptions. There I was thinking she was having a great time, sitting there so beautifully and peacefully, but the truth was that she was struggling just as much, if not more, than I was.

This was a sobering experience for me—and I suspect we all do things like this more often than we'd like to admit. For example, maybe we see couples on social media looking happy and perfect, while our own relationship is filled with arguments and difficulty. We keep seeing all these happy couples doing things together, all of them looking like the perfect couple.

But don't be fooled; things are seldom as they seem on the surface.

We cannot take things at face value or constantly compare our lives to those of others. The truth is that we never know what's going on with anyone. Even our closest friends may be hiding dark secrets, addictions, or pains. In fact, it's quite possible that the happiest people we see day in and day out are actually the most depressed or anxious. Of course, this may not *always* be the case, but again, who knows?

If we see another person's life and envy it, wishing we were them, we should be very careful. We may get exactly what we wish for.

Take Robin Williams, for example. He was hilarious and always had the ability to make everybody around him laugh. It seemed as though he was the happiest guy ever, and I'm sure many of us would've loved to have the good life we assumed he had. Yet as we learned with his unfortunate death, the happy life we all imagined perhaps was not as happy as it seemed.

At the end of the day, the truth of universal suffering stands true. Everybody suffers, and all of us put on a multitude of masks in order to seem socially acceptable. No matter how great someone's life may seem to be, the truth is that we may never know the struggles they experience.

Don't make assumptions about other people, and don't wish for their life, because the truth is that things are seldom as they seem.

NO SELF,
NO PROBLEM

When we see beyond self, we no longer
cling to happiness and we can truly be
happy.

—AJAHN CHAH

WHENEVER THERE IS suffering in our lives
there is always a sense that someone—an
unchanging, individual self—is experiencing
that suffering. In fact, suffering is born out of this
concept of "self." When there is belief in a self,
attachments and aversions are naturally created,
allowing our likes and dislikes to start governing our thoughts, actions, and speech. We end
up wanting what we don't have, or having what
we don't want, leaving us constantly dissatisfied.
Even when we finally get what we want, we are
still in an anxious state, fearing the inevitable

loss of our impermanent attainment. We protect this sense of self at all costs, living life constantly chasing pleasure and security, while desperately avoiding discomfort and insecurity. Living our lives in this way allows no room for peace, joy, and contentment.

The Buddha investigated this problem of suffering and found the solution: *anatta*. *Anatta*, which again typically translates as "no-self," is the understanding that we are not as solid or separate as we may think. Don't agree? Well, where is this *self* we believe ourselves to be? Most would say they are their body, but this can't be true because our body is constantly changing, and most of its functions are not even under our control.

We are not the ones consciously growing our nails or digesting our food, and we sure as hell don't ask to be sick or feel pain, yet these things are constantly happening to our body. Furthermore, many people have lost limbs, had organ transplants, and cut their hair without any loss of self. We may then think we are our thoughts and emotions, yet upon deeper investigation of this we find we have no more control over them than we do the weather. The mind constantly moves around and out of our control with fantasies, daydreams, cravings, judgments, aversions, etc., all coming with a juicy set of emotions that make them seem all the more real.

All our lives seem to be happening to a single, separate self, yet upon searching for it, it becomes more and more mysterious and elusive.

It's important to understand that having no solid, separate self doesn't mean there's a void or that we don't exist. Clearly we are here experiencing life.

The truth of anatta is not meant to be nihilistic or turn us into nothing, but rather used as a sign that points to our liberation from suffering. One common Buddhist analogy illustrates this well.

Imagine a man walks into a dark shed and sees a snake. Frozen with fear, his mind fills with thoughts about the snake attacking him and how he needs to kill it or escape before being bit. In this moment his fear is very real, as is the snake, but when he turns the light on in the shed, he discovers the snake is only an old rope curled up on the floor. Immediately his suffering is relieved with the realization that there never really was a snake at all. Now every time he goes into the shed, he knows the rope is only a rope, not a snake, and he has no fear. When his friends enter the shed and become frozen with fear, he has compassion and simply explains that it's only a rope. Some believe him and extinguish their fear immediately, while others still aren't sure and continue to suffer every time they enter the shed. In the same way, our sense of self seems so real with its thoughts and emotions, yet when we realize there is no self who owns them, our suffering is extinguished.

Another common example of this is going to the movies. For the hour or two in which we are watching the movie, we are heavily involved with the emotions of the characters. We may get angry or even cry, losing ourselves in the drama. But at the end of the day, we all know it's not real. Leonardo DiCaprio didn't really die in the ocean after the Titanic sank, but for that short period of time we believed it enough to shed some tears. (Don't judge me; you know you cried too.)

Of course, realizing there is no self is much easier said than done.

We are very much attached to this idea of a self. We don't just hear the teaching of anatta and magically understand. It takes many years of meditation and mindfully observing our attachments to our thoughts, sensations, and emotions before we start to loosen the grip of this deeply rooted belief in a self, but it's worth the journey.

Don't just take my words and believe or not believe. Investigate the suffering in your life thoroughly.

THE
CONTROL
CENTER

*Delight in heedfulness. Guard your thoughts
well.*

—BUDDHA

AWARENESS IS A great tool for coming into
the present moment without judgment, but
having a nonjudgmental attitude doesn't mean
that we don't have discernment. Awareness has
the ability to discern between the varieties of life.
For instance, awareness knows the difference
between hot and cold. Even without thinking
about it, we can easily know from a direct experience if something is hot or cold. Before we begin
to judge or label the experience, we just simply
know. It's not a judgment, but rather a discernment of what *is*.

Imagine our awareness as someone sitting at the control center of our mind. Before it takes the controls, we've given it specific instructions on which states of mind are allowed to take control and which aren't. Our awareness stays on the lookout for harmful states of mind that will cause problems if they take the head seat at the control center. If awareness falls asleep, even for a moment, any state of mind can come in and start controlling your actions, speech, and thoughts.

Most people don't have their awareness in the head seat at the control center. This means that any reactions that arise will take full control of their being. If awareness isn't there discerning the character of the visitors, surely chaos will ensue. Without awareness, anger, for example, could come along and take over our control system, making us act according to its wishes. But if we instead have our awareness manning the station, it can see the anger come and allow it to be there without letting it take control.

With a steady meditation practice, we build awareness of ourselves throughout the day. We know what state of mind we are in at each moment. We learn which emotions and thoughts are present and are able to discern which can be held on to and which we can let go. A good guide to knowing which to let in and which to let go of is *ahimsa, or* nonviolence. We must ask ourselves if this thought or emotion will bring harm to others or ourselves. If so, we can let it go.

Please don't think mindfulness practice means we passively watch our lives pass us by without engaging in them. Nonjudgmental awareness means coming or acting from a place of acceptance, clarity, and wisdom—using discernment instead of ignorance. If we can understand the current situation we are in and see it clearly with our awareness, then we can use our awareness as a tool to bring the most appropriate action for that moment. Instead of letting whatever arises take over, we can allow our awareness to take the head seat at the control center of our minds.

PRACTICING WITH ADDICTIONS

Addiction is the only prison where the locks are on the inside.

—ANONYMOUS

AN ADDICTION IS a strong urge or craving toward a certain habit, behavior, compulsion, or thinking pattern. With an addiction, one becomes enslaved to a substance or action that brings about a particular reward, typically, but not always, a euphoric one. It's important to understand that addictions are not limited only to drugs, alcohol, food, and sex, but can also be found in negative thought patterns, views of oneself, ideas about people, beliefs about life, and so on. The bottom line is that most of us have an addiction to something that makes us feel stuck and oftentimes overwhelmed. This may make it seem as though freedom and liberation are not an option.

Although it might seem hopeless, it is possible to work through an addiction of any severity. By understanding our addiction, and with the help of meditation, mindfulness, supportive friends, and perhaps a therapist and rehab, we can begin to free ourselves from the shackles binding us to our addiction. In my years of studying my own mind and those of clients and friends with addictions, I have found there to be two main aspects of an addiction that keep us locked in its seductive grip:

- The feelings we don't want to feel, which started the whole pattern of addiction to begin with.
- The cravings for the feelings we do want to feel, which are generally trying to escape or ease the ones we'd rather not feel.

In most cases, there are certain emotions, thoughts, or feelings that seem too overwhelming or painful to face. Some examples are loneliness, emptiness, depression, anxiety, fear, and grief. When these feelings enter our being, it may appear as though they will never go away—as if we will have to experience them for the rest of our lives. This is when the addictive behavior makes sense. "I don't like how I feel, and it doesn't seem like it's going to just magically go away, so I need to do _____ to feel better." We can fill in the blank with our particular escape method or methods. Although it may seem like certain feelings will never go away, this is truly a false belief. Feelings, thoughts, emotions, and sensations come and go throughout the day. Nothing is ever static, and if we begin to pay attention with mindfulness, we will find that everything changes all the time. Please note that this does not mean that certain feelings or thoughts will not reoccur many times throughout the day; it just means that they will come and go like clouds passing through the vast, open sky.

For a person wrestling with an addiction, it's important to get in touch with these underlying feelings and cravings running the addiction, so as to learn to have the courage to stay with the discomfort, rather than immediately trying to flee. Meditation is a useful tool for this, as it teaches you to stay in an open and relaxed way with whatever may be happening in the moment. By continuously facing and allowing these uncomfortable feelings to stay there, we are slowly releasing ourselves from their powerful grip.

Over a long period of time the feelings, which once seemed unbearable and unfaceable, will become gradually more manageable and spacious, but please don't expect results quickly. I faced feelings of emptiness, hopelessness, and anxiety for about five or six years, until finally, one day, after years of opening to it over and over again, I started to see it dissipate.

I am reminded of the movie *The Shawshank Redemption*, in which Andy Dufresne, after years of scraping pebbles from his prison wall, finally broke through and escaped. Every time we are able to stay with the discomfort, we are like Andy, slowly scraping a few more pebbles from the prison wall of addiction. If we keep facing the feelings and cravings—feeling them fully without acting on them—then we will eventually escape from our personal prison of addiction.

THERE IS NO
WAY TO PEACE

*Peace begins with you by the actions you
do every day and the way you live your
life. Peace is a choice, and you promote
peace wherever you go.*

—JIM SCHNEIDER

IT IS GENERALLY understood that meditation
is a way of attaining peace, and many believe
this peace will come only after many years of
intense, dedicated practice. As a meditation
instructor, I find most people come to meditation believing this to be true. It is quite natural
for those starting on this path to feel as though
meditation will give them something that will
somehow fix or clean up the messiness of their
lives, and through much effort they will no longer
experience their pain, anger, depression, anxiety,

confusion, or cravings. Many of us have this subtle hope that our meditation practice will lead to
some ultimate comfort, security, and satisfaction. Unfortunately, the truth of the matter is as
Suzuki Roshi used to say: "Not always so."

"There is no way to peace" says Thich Nhat
Hanh, "Peace is the way."

I find this saying profound, and only recently
started to feel as though I am beginning to truly
appreciate and understand its message. The way
to peace is unattainable—not because it doesn't
exist, but rather because it must be something we
bring to each moment of our lives. Peace is gentleness, compassion, and wisdom actualized right
smack in the middle of ordinary, everyday living.
Peace is literally the way.

Meditation is not a means to gain peace, but
rather a way to practice bringing peace to whatever is occurring in that moment. I am not saying
meditation does not bring about tranquility and
inner calm, but the feelings from deeper meditative states naturally dissipate like an early morning fog on a sunny day. The warm fuzzy feelings
come and go; nothing can ever be static in an
ever-changing universe. If we believe peace is
only a feeling we must attain and maintain, it will

always be waxing and waning, but as we mature on our meditative path, we find peace to be what we choose to bring to every moment.

Understanding peace in this way allows our meditation practice to become the training ground where we are able to bring peace to ourselves—*all* of ourselves. By sitting with our monkey mind, difficult emotions, body pains, and storylines—without judgments or labels—we are actually bringing peace to our entire being.

Naturally this begins flowing into each moment of everyday life, such as doing the dishes, being stuck in a traffic jam, working, eating, going to the bathroom, and so on. Instead of waiting for peace, our life becomes *our actualized expression* and embodiment of peace, moment by moment. We eventually realize peace doesn't necessarily mean feeling good (although sometimes it does!), but rather is our approach to all the circumstances we experience in our lives.

There is a blameless joy that arises from practicing peace.

Try it out and see for yourself!

IN SUMMARY

It's been a hell of a run. But all good things must come to an end.

—BRAD KERN

IN THIS concluding chapter, I'd like to offer a summary of the themes of this book—distilled into the principles that have come to guide me throughout my life and allowed me to experience deep joy and appreciation for it.

I UNDERSTAND LIFE IS RARE AND PRECIOUS; I REFUSE TO WASTE IT.

Our lives truly are rare and precious. In Buddhism, there is an analogy of attaining a human birth that goes something like this. Imagine a planet the same size as Earth completely covered in water—one great ocean. Floating on the top of the ocean is one small inner tube. Swimming in the depths is one blind turtle, which comes up once every hundred years to take a breath. The chances of being born a human being are the same chances as that one turtle popping up with its head right in the middle of that inner tube. Slim indeed.

We must understand how rare this life is and how many things in the entire universe have come together perfectly in such a way so that we can be here in this moment. Had the Earth been a little closer or further away from the sun, we wouldn't exist. The entire universe is functioning so we can take a breath right now. When we realize how strange and awesome this life is, we will not want to waste it. With this deeper understanding we will want to explore the mystery of life that we are and be of some use to those around us.

I KNOW DEATH IS CERTAIN AND THE TIME OF DEATH IS UNCERTAIN; I DON'T IGNORANTLY BELIEVE I HAVE TIME. EVERY DAY IS A GIFT; THERE MAY NOT BE A TOMORROW.

Understanding the preciousness of life is the first step to living deeply, but more important than this understanding is realizing that we will surely die. Our culture rarely talks much about death. Many times when I begin giving talks about death and impermanence, people become very uncomfortable, or don't want to hear it. Imagine the looks I get when I tell them to contemplate death five times a day to become happier . . .

But the truth is death and dying are very real parts of this life and they need to be thought about. If we don't understand death, we will not truly live. If we think we have time, then there's time to waste. When we realize our time is running out, we slow down and appreciate things as they are. It will help us understand that just this moment is enough for joy and ease.

I'VE REALIZED THE ONLY THINGS I CAN CONTROL ARE MY WORDS AND ACTIONS, AND HOW I CHOOSE TO RESPOND TO WHAT LIFE OFFERS ME. I ALSO KNOW FOR CERTAIN, I CANNOT ESCAPE THE CONSEQUENCES OF MY CHOICES.

Most of us crave control, but most of the time we are busy trying to control things we have absolutely no control over. The only things we can control are our words and actions and how we choose to respond to what life offers us. We don't need to neurotically try to control our lives, but instead can focus our attention on speaking and acting kindly and compassionately. We can also practice opening up to our lives just the way they are, allowing for true peace and joy. It's also important to realize that we cannot escape the consequences of our actions. If we want wholesome results, we must practice wholesome ways of being in the world.

I'VE SEEN FIRSTHAND HOW GETTING WHAT I WANT IS NEVER PERMANENTLY FULFILLING. EVERYTHING CHANGES, AND "WANTING" NEVER ENDS.

Think about how often we have received exactly what we have wanted from life. Are we ultimately fulfilled yet? Have we stopped wanting? Recently, I asked this question of a ninety-year-old woman during a workshop at a senior home. She answered no. Let's not wait until we are ninety to realize that the wanting mind is never satisfied. Instead let's practice contentment day in and day out, being at ease with what we already have. This is the path to freedom.

I SEE HOW THE GREATEST JOY AND MEANING COME FROM RELIEVING SUFFERING IN OTHERS. I ALSO KNOW THE JOY OF BEING KIND AND LOVING, EVEN WHEN THE REST OF THE WORLD IS NOT.

Being kind feels good. Helping others is an infinite source of joy. Most of our suffering comes from focusing too much on what we want (or don't want). If we shift our focus to helping others, we will feel joyful all the time. Even when others are not being kind or loving back, there is a blameless joy in acting wholesomely in our daily lives.

> **I UNDERSTAND THAT THIS IS IT. THERE IS NO OTHER TIME, NO OTHER LIFE. IF I DON'T PRACTICE BEING AT EASE NOW, THEN I WILL NEVER BE AT EASE. JUST THIS IS ENOUGH FOR TRUE CONTENTMENT.**

Let's not waste our lives chasing after some fantasy reality on the other side of the rainbow. There is no other side of the rainbow; there is only this life as it is now. This body, this mind, the family we have, the situations in which we find ourselves, the difficulties and sorrows we have—this is it. This is our life and this is the only thing we can experience and work with. Let's put all our attention on bringing peace and gentleness to our actual lives and continue our journey to becoming a truly authentic human being.

The beauty of having a meditation practice is that it includes everything. Nothing is left out. This radical and inclusive approach to our lives and ourselves is not only liberating but also necessary during these times of aggression and violence to both our planet and each other. The world is screaming for us to cultivate kindness, compassion, and wisdom. We need brave spiritual warriors who can face the discomforts of fear, aggression, and hatred without becoming ensnared by them— people who are comfortable with discomfort and are able to transform the seductive grips of power and control into the wisdom of peace and harmony. Although at times it may seem impossible, softening our hearts is always a possibility, and with the clarity and stability gained from continued meditation practice, all of us can experience spontaneity and right action amid each unique difficulty life presents to us. We must start right here, right now, exactly where we are, with our own hearts and minds. We must learn to trust ourselves. If we don't work on ourselves, we cannot face the terrors of the outside world.

As our individual practice comes to fruition, our compassion and wisdom will spread naturally to all we encounter, teaching others the way through example. Everything we do eventually becomes an expression of our meditation practice. The world *will* notice it.

Please don't disregard the power of meditation—of literally taking time each day to pay attention and do nothing—simply be. Practicing doing nothing is what has given my life everything, and I hope that by sharing this book with all of you, you will receive the true peace and joy of a dedicated practice, and you will come to realize that your life is in fact meditation.

As always, I wish you well on your journey.

ACKNOWLEDGMENTS

I AM INDEBTED TO the many enlightened individuals, both past and present, who have blessed me with the gift of their wisdom, teachings, and inspiration. I am grateful to those who have contributed to the changes I have made in my own life, some of whom I've had the honor to meet, and others who have spoken to me through the pages of their own insightful books. I would be remiss if I didn't personally acknowledge them here and thank them for their guidance and inspiration:

To my wife, Michelle, my son, Mason, and my daughters, Madelyn and Emmeline, for their love, support, and inspiration.

To Heart Circle Sangha and my current teacher, Joan Hogetsu Hoeberichts, for helping me continuously deepen my practice.

To Dharma Drum Retreat Center, which has allowed me the silence and solitude necessary to cultivate mindfulness, wisdom, and peace.

To Simon Child, Chang Wen Fashi, Pema Chödrön, Jack Kornfield, Thich Nhat Hanh, Ajahn

Brahm, Dzigar Kongtrül, Eckhart Tolle, and many other like-minded teachers for their inspiring words and for encouraging me to continue with my practice of wisdom and compassion.

To Buddha, Master Sheng Yen, Chögyam Trungpa Rinpoche, Ajahn Chah, and all other deceased teachers who have passed their wisdom down throughout the generations.

To David Gettis, my first publisher, close friend, and editor, for his constant dedication and hard work on all of my writing endeavors.

To all friends and family for all their love and support.

ABOUT THE AUTHOR

 MARK VAN BUREN is a mindful-living trainer, yoga/meditation instructor, personal trainer, and musician who has been promoting health and wellness for over a decade. He has run dozens of workshops and retreats all over the Tri-State Area.

He has worked extensively with children and adults with autism and other special needs and has even released two solo albums, based on his inward journey through meditation, under the band name "Seeking the Seeker." Van Buren holds a bachelor of arts in religious studies from Montclair State University and two associate degrees from Bergen Community College, in exercise science and music.

WHAT TO READ NEXT FROM WISDOM PUBLICATIONS

A Fool's Guide to Actual Happiness
Mark Van Buren

This book allows you to explore who you are—warts and all—and gives you tools to love and accept what you find.

Buddhism for Dudes
A Jarhead's Field Guide to Mindfulness
Gerry Stribling

"*Buddhism for Dudes* shoots straight and doesn't blink. It's John Wayne meets Zen, complete with all the wisdom and tough-guy charm you'd expect."
—Matthew Bortolin, author of *The Dharma of Star Wars*

Saltwater Buddha
A Surfer's Quest to Find Zen on the Sea
Jaimal Yogis

"Heartfelt, honest, and deceptively simple. It's great stuff with the words 'Cult Classic' stamped all over it."
—Alex Wade, author of *Surf Nation*

I Wanna Be Well
How a Punk Found Peace and You Can Too
Miguel Chen with Rod Meade Sperry

"Much in the spirit of *Dharma Punx*, *Get in the Van*, or even *Please Kill Me*, Miguel Chen has done something important with this book. And I'm gonna stop feeling self-conscious about listening to DRI while doing yoga." —Zach Blair, guitarist for Rise Against

The Death of You

A Book for Anyone Who Might Not Live Forever
Miguel Chen

"With a cheerful balance of reverence and irreverence, this book is a joy to read — and Miguel is such a good teacher." — Cyndi Lee, author of *Yoga Body, Buddha Mind*

About Wisdom Publications

Wisdom Publications is the leading publisher of classic and contemporary Buddhist books and practical works on mindfulness. To learn more about us or to explore our other books, please visit our website at wisdomexperience.org or contact us at the address below.

Wisdom Publications
199 Elm Street
Somerville, MA 02144 USA

We are a 501(c)(3) organization, and donations in support of our mission are tax deductible.

Wisdom Publications is affiliated with the Foundation for the Preservation of the Mahayana Tradition (FPMT).